Minnesota Weather

Richard A. Keen

American & World Geographic Publishing

To Helena
and Samantha, Amada, Michael, Daniel, and Sarah
and Mouse, Wombat, and even Shadow

© 1992 American & World
Geographic Publishing
P.O. Box 5630
Helena, MT 59604
Text © 1992 Richard A. Keen
ISBN 1-56037-000-9

**Library of Congress Cataloging-in-
Publication Data**
Keen, Richard A.
Minnesota weather / Richard A. Keen.
    p.   cm.
    Includes bibliographical references and
    index.
    ISBN 1-56037-000-9 : $14.95
1. Minnesota--Climate.   I. Title.
QC984.M6K44   1992
551.69776--dc20

Front cover, inset: *Puffy cumulus clouds,
typical of Minnesota's many fine summer
days, dot the sky near Chanhassen.*
MIKE MAGNUSON PHOTO

Background: *The heaviest snowstorm in
Minnesota history buried Excelsior, along
with most of the rest of eastern Minnesota,
under two feet and more of snow at the
beginning of November 1991.*
MIKE MAGNUSON PHOTO

ACKNOWLEDGMENTS

Minnesotans always have something—and often quite a bit—to say about their weather. Some think it's wonderful year-round. To many, though, summer means four months of bad sledding, while others enjoy summer not because it's warm but because it brings the spectacle of thunder, lightning and tornadoes.

All those individuals who shared their experiences, enthusiasm, and varied points of view made their contribution to *Minnesota Weather.* I'm especially grateful to several "weather buffs," including Bruce Watson, who provided me with a wealth of data about the weather of the Twin Cites and the state; Tom St. Martin, whose massive "Summary of St. Paul Climatological Data" I thumbed through hundreds of times; Scott Woelm and Roger Jensen for their tornado tales; and Bob King, Max Radloff, and other members of the Arrowhead and Minnesota astronomical societies for their photos and stories about eclipses and auroras.

I also appreciate the efforts by the people of those government agencies that deal with the weather, including the National Oceanic and Atmospheric Administration (NOAA), the United States Forest Service, the Minnesota Geological Survey, and the Minnesota Department of Natural Resources. Special thanks go to Greg Spoden, Minnesota's Assistant State Climatologist, and Jon Eischeid, who supplied disks of NOAA's state climate data. Minnesota also has a wonderful collection of libraries and historical societies, among which the Minnesota, Carlton County, and Otter Tail County historical societies, and Duluth's Canal Park Marine Museum, were particularly helpful.

Overall, I thoroughly enjoyed writing *Minnesota Weather,* and value the acquaintances I made among Minnesota's weather buffs. There was one major disappointment, however. Dozens of Minnesotans—amateur and professional photographers, along with weather buffs who happen to have a camera—sent me hundreds of outstanding photos of thunderstorms, snow, lightning, auroras and anything else to do with the weather. I wish we could have printed them all but, sadly, we couldn't. So my final kudos goes to all those who took the time to send photos but won't have the reward of seeing them in print. Their efforts are sincerely appreciated—thanks!

CONTENTS

Maps, Charts and Graphs

MINNESOTA'S
PLACE IN THE ATMOSPHERE

■■■■■■■■■■■■■■■■■■■■■■■■■■■■

On the east side of Cleveland Avenue in Roseville, less than a mile south of Interstate 35W, sits a stone monument with a brass plaque marking the "Forty-fifth parallel of north latitude...which is exactly one-half the distance between the equator and the North Pole." Midway between the equator and the North Pole—no wonder Minnesota's weather is the way it is! Swinging between arctic onslaughts in the winter, tropical heat in the summer, and plenty of simply pleasant weather in between, Roseville, along with the rest of Minnesota, has one of the most volatile and invigorating climates in the world.

Latitude is certainly not the only factor that shapes the weather and climate of Minnesota. Sharing the same latitude as places in Minnesota are rain forests along the coast of Oregon, the arid, dusty chill of Mongolia's Gobi Desert, and the temperate vineyards of France. Unlike Oregon and France, Minnesota sits in the middle of the continent, with land extending for a thousand or more miles in every direction. Free from the moderating influences of the world's oceans, Minnesotans are accustomed to 100° summertime heat and subzero cold during the winter—extremes seldom seen in France or along Oregon's coast.

Mongolia, the home of Genghis Khan, may seem remote and exotic, but Genghis Khan and Paul Bunyan actually endured much the same range of temperatures! But Mongolia is a dry and dusty place, even drier than Minnesota was during the "Dust Bowl" years of the 1930s. Mongolia's drought is also permanent, and the reason lies in the hills. Mongolia is surrounded on all sides by mile-high mountains, with the world's greatest mountains—the five-mile-high Himalayas—lying to the south. These peaks and ridges effectively block the flow of moisture-laden air that might otherwise stream in from the tropical seas to the south and east of Asia. Minnesota, on the other hand, has only the Ozark Mountains between it and the state's primary moisture source, the Gulf of Mexico. Needless to say, the Ozarks are much less formidable a barrier than are the Himalayas, and air that can't get over the Ozarks has no trouble going around them! This ready, if not steady, supply of moisture-laden gulf air provides Minnesota with enough rain and snow to keep the farms productive and the lakes full (most of the time).

In a way, it's strange that it rains (or snows) at all in Minnesota. Most of the earth between 30° and 60° north latitude (as well as 30° to 60° south) lies in the zone of the "prevailing westerlies." This band includes all of Minnesota, and, actually, all of the United States except southern Florida, Hawaii, and parts of Alaska. In this zone fair- and foul-weather systems move from west to east. But if the winds always blew in this direction, wet air from the Gulf of Mexico would never waft north to feed rain storms for Minnesota's lakes and farms. The air that streams in off the Pacific Ocean is moist enough, but most of that moisture is lost to the rainforests of the Pacific Coast and the snowfields of the Rockies. By the time Pacific air reaches eastern Montana and the Dakotas it is quite dry, and usually brings mild, sunny weather to Minnesota rather than rain or snow. Fortunately, the prevailing westerlies (westerly winds blow from the west) are the most fickle winds in the world, and may actually blow from any direction, including straight up or down! The prevailing westerlies may be thought of as a broad stream of air that circles the globe at about the latitude of Minnesota. During the summer this stream moves north into Canada, and in wintertime it shifts a few hundred miles south. Embedded in this broad stream are smaller whirls and eddies, and the stream itself may—like the Mississippi River—meander into bends and bows thousands of miles long.

CYCLONES & ANTICYCLONES

The broad flow of the prevailing westerlies looks quite impressive on global weather charts, but it is really the little whirls and eddies that do most of the work. These whirls are the low and high pressure systems, also known (respectively) as cyclones and anticyclones, that bring stormy and fair weather in an ever-changing sequence. The word "cyclone" comes from the Greek *kyklos,* meaning "circle." So, the air in a cyclone blows in a circular pattern around the center. However, this circular motion can be in either a clockwise or counter-clockwise direction. By definition, and to avoid confusion, the air in cyclones blows counter-clockwise (as seen from above), while in "anticyclones" the flow is clockwise. (In the southern hemisphere, the flow is reversed, with cyclones blowing clockwise and anticyclones counter-clockwise—which has nothing to do with Minnesota, of course, but some of you are bound to be curious about this.) In terms of air pressure—that number you read off your barometer—cyclones are centers of low pressure, and anticyclones have high pressure (this is true in both the northern and southern hemispheres). Low pressure is, in essence, a partial vacuum, so air will stream into a cyclone from surrounding areas of higher pressure (or anticyclones). Putting all these motions together, air spirals outward from the center of a high-pressure anticyclone, and spirals inward toward the center of a low-pressure cyclone. Cyclones come in all sizes, from tiny whirlwinds like dust devils (which are miniature low pressure systems) to enormous regions of low pressure that may cover half a continent. In the Midwest, "cyclone" often means a tornado, and tornadoes are definitely small and intense cyclones. In Australia and India, folks think of cyclones as hurricanes. However, meteorologists around the world usually think of cyclones as storm systems that are several hundred to a thousand miles across. These are the storms that bring snowstorms in the winter and all-day rains in the spring and summer.

Cyclones are marvels of natural engineering, and perform a variety of necessary functions. On the global scale, a major task of the atmosphere (along with giving us something to breathe) is to equalize the earth's temperature by shipping hot air to the poles and cold air back to the tropics. If this didn't happen, the unequal solar heating of different parts of the planet would heat the tropics until they literally boiled and chill the arctic regions until the air itself froze. Fortunately, the large temperature differences get air currents moving, much like the currents that develop in a heated pot of water. In the tropics such things as the trade winds (the winds that sway Hawaiian and Caribbean palm trees) and equatorial thunderstorms move the warm and cool air around. Up here in Minnesota, along with most everywhere else between the tropics and the arctic, cyclones do the job. Their counter-clockwise rotation (in the northern hemisphere) draws tropical air northward around the eastern side of the storm, and cold air southward on the west side.

MAJOR STORM TRACKS OF NORTH AMERICA
Solid lines show the main storm tracks

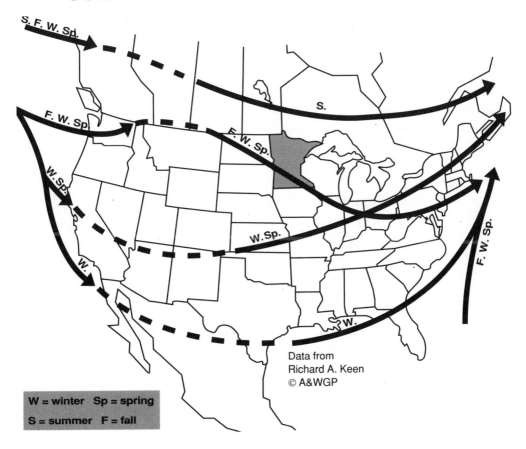

Data from
Richard A. Keen
© A&WGP

W = winter Sp = spring
S = summer F = fall

As the swirling and mixing of warm and cold air within a cyclone equalizes the global climate, it also gives us weather. Cyclones nearly always form along the boundary between arctic air to the north and subtropical air to the south. The importance of these boundaries was recognized by Norwegian meteorologists shortly after World War I. With the war fresh in their minds, they named the boundaries "fronts," and to this day fronts are depicted on weather maps in a nearly identical manner to battle fronts drawn on a map of the Somme. Indeed, fronts are battle zones, with the clashing air masses creating turmoil far greater than any that humans can lay claim to.

FRONTS

There are four basic kinds of fronts. Before a cyclone develops, the boundary between the opposing air masses may lie still for a while. These "stationary fronts" are usually fairly tranquil places with slow-moving patches of light rain or snow resulting in protracted spells of drizzly weather. However, the weather may turn anything but tranquil if the air on the warm side of the front is exceptionally moist, and heavy slow-moving thunderstorms pop up, unleashing torrential rains and flash floods.

As the cyclone starts spinning, the stationary front starts moving. A "warm front" marks the leading edge of northbound warm air, while arctic air plunges south behind a "cold front." Warm and cold fronts are *not* tranquil places. Of the two, cold fronts are usually more exciting. Being heavier, the cold air shoves like a wedge beneath the warm, and usually more moist, air mass. Forced upward, the warm air expands and cools, and its load of water vapor condenses into a cloud of tiny water droplets or ice crystals. Ultimately, these drops and crystals grow into rain and snow. Ahead of cold fronts the forced uplift may be great enough to produce thunderstorms and, sometimes, tornadoes. Along warm fronts the warm air overruns the cold air to its north, and its rising motion is normally gentler than along a cold front. This produces more moderate, but longer-lasting, rain- and snowfalls. Although not as intense as cold-front storms, warm fronts may produce greater total rain or snow (many of Minnesota's biggest snow storms result from warm fronts).

The final member of this menagerie of fronts is the "occluded front," whose name comes from the Latin for (roughly) "shut out" or "cut off." After a cyclone has been spinning around for a day or two, the (usually) faster-moving cold front starts catching up to the warm front. Both fronts move spoke-like around the low pressure center, and the "warm sector," the wedge of warm air caught between the cold and warm fronts, shrinks as the cyclone develops. Eventually the fronts merge, completely lifting the warm sector off the ground. With the warm air "cut off" from the ground, the fronts become an occluded front, an indistinct boundary between two similarly cold air masses. Several thousand feet up, however, warm air is still being shoved around by cold air, and rain and snow are still being made.

■■■■■■■■■■■■■■■

MINNESOTA STORM CYCLES

Every year 30 or 40 cyclones pass directly over Minnesota, and as many more brush by close enough to drop rain or snow on some part of the state. That comes out to one or two a week, which means that every five days, on the average, Minnesota's weather does a complete swing from clear to rain (or snow) and back to clear, and from cold to warm to cold again.

It's not an even cycle, however. Weeks may pass, especially during the summer and early fall, without a significant cyclone affecting Minnesota's weather. At these times a huge high-pressure over the western Atlantic Ocean—the famous Bermuda High of summer—expands north and west, and Minnesota sweats in persistent heat. If the air is humid enough, the pattern may break locally from scattered thunderstorms, and occasional weak cold fronts may dip south into Minnesota, but most of the cyclones pass by well to the north.

Cyclones may become equally rare in mid-winter, but now because they pass too far south. This happens when a massive arctic high sits over Canada and the northern plains, including Minnesota, and the North Star State sits cold, clear, and dry.

During the in-between seasons, however, cyclones are a way of life in Minnesota. October and April rains, November and March blizzards, and May and June tornadoes all mark the passage of the main storm track across Minnesota.

There are several main storm tracks across North America, and they vary from season to season. The Gulf Coast storm track that dominates in mid-winter is too far south to concern Minnesotans. Most of Minnesota's cyclones have one of two distinct origins: the "Colorado lows" that form over the southern Rockies and track northeast, and the "Alberta clippers" that drive southeast from their origins over the northern Rockies. The Alberta storms bring light rain or snow followed by arctic blasts, while the Colorado lows bring up moist air from the Gulf of Mexico and may become heavy snowstorms.

Not all storms follow these tracks, mind you, but they give an idea of where most storms come from and where they go. Keep in mind that cyclones may buck the prevailing westerlies and move out of the south or east, and some of Minnesota's worst storms have wandered in bizarre curlicue paths or just simply stalled over the state. It is this infinite variety of storms that makes Minnesota's weather what it is: ever-changing, sometimes terrifying and sometimes delightful, but always fascinating.

HOT & COLD

■■■■■■■■■■■■■■■■■■■■■■■■■■■■

Everybody knows it gets cold in Minnesota. Many times each winter places like International Falls, Hibbing, Roseau, Bemidji, Warroad, and Embarrass earn a day's fame as the coldest place in the Union. It's no wonder that Frostbite Falls, legendary home of Bullwinkle the Moose, was placed in Minnesota. Less well known, especially outside of Minnesota, is how hot it can get. Minnesota's all-time high temperature of 115° is well above the records for such tropical paradises as Hawaii and Florida, and the Twin Cities high of 108° beats any heat ever recorded in Albuquerque, New Mexico; Tombstone, Arizona; and Washington, D.C., and even exceeds such global hot spots as Beirut, Saigon, and Havana (but not Baghdad!). However, Minnesota's cold days are more impressive than its hot ones, so let's start at the bottom of the thermometer.

There's more than a little competition among Minnesota's towns about which is the state's, or even the nation's, Ice Box. You might think that all I'd have to do is rattle off a few numbers, point out that Frostbite Falls is obviously the coldest, and settle the issue for once and for all. Of course, if weather were so simple, there'd be no need to write a book about it! Weather statistics are much like baseball statistics, and asking what's the coldest place in Minnesota is like asking who is the best hitter in the American League. Do you take batting averages, home runs, or runs batted in to rate the players? So it is with temperatures: do you take average yearly temperatures, average winter low temperatures, or all-time extreme cold readings? Let's check them all, plus a few more...

Comparative averages should be computed over the same time period; otherwise, subtle changes in the climate may load the dice in favor of one place over another. Right now, the standard averaging period is 1951 through 1980. This gives a 30-year average, the world standard for such things. By 1993, these will be replaced by 1961 through 1990 averages, but those aren't available yet.

THE NATION'S ICEBOX?

Minnesota's lowest average yearly temperature belongs to Roseau, at 35.3°—just 3° above freezing! Close behind are Warroad (35.7°), Baudette (35.9°), and International Falls

MINNESOTA'S GREATEST HEAT WAVE
Moorhead, Minn. July, 1936

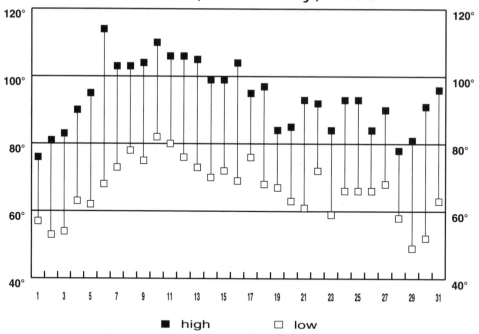

■ high   □ low

MINNESOTA'S GREATEST COLD WAVE
Leech Lake, Minn. Jan.-Feb. 1899

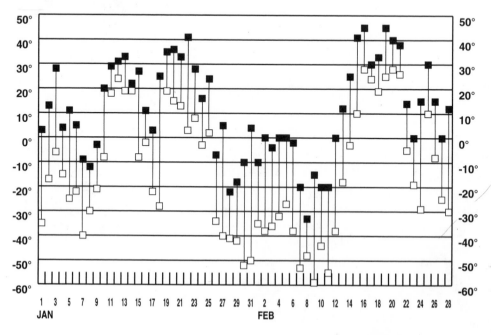

Data from U.S. Weather Bureau
© A&WGP

(36.2°). International Falls has the distinction of being the coldest major National Weather Service station in the "lower 48" states. As a major station, "The Falls" reports its readings every hour, while the other three stations check in once or twice a day. This doesn't affect the reality of the temperatures, but it does influence how quickly and widely the temperature readings are reported. While International Falls makes the news, Roseau is one degree colder, on the average. Roseau is not the coldest place in the nation, however. Across the Red River in North Dakota, Langdon averages 35.0°, one third of a degree lower than Roseau. To find colder places we must go up in elevation (Mt. Washington, New Hampshire, averages 26.6°) or north (Barrow, Alaska, averages a mere 9.0°).

Roseau also takes the cake for average winter temperatures. Its average January low temperature, 12.4° below zero, is *the* lowest in the United States (outside of Alaska). It's 0.7° colder than Warroad and Langdon, and 10° lower than Mt. Washington. Roseau's thermometer dips to zero—the temperature at which snow squeaks—or lower on 69 nights a year). However, Roseau's overall average January temperature (day and night) is 0.1° higher than Langdon's. Now you can see why assigning "Nation's Ice Box" status is so tricky!

Yet another measure of coldness, and one that means a lot to anyone who grows trees and other perennial plants, is the long-term average of the lowest temperature recorded each winter. The U.S. Department of Agriculture has translated these average annual minimum temperatures into "plant hardiness zones," meaning that plants that can handle 30° below winters may not survive where 40° below zero is recorded. On the USDA Plant Hardiness Zone Map issued in 1990, Minnesota harbors three regions marked "Zone 2b." In Zone 2b, the coldest temperature recorded in a typical winter is in the -40° to -45° range (no bananas here!). One of these areas covers much of Beltrami and Lake of the Woods counties, while another is in northeastern St. Louis County. The third area of Zone 2b is a small patch along the Canadian border, north of—you guessed it—Roseau. Outside of interior Alaska and a few isolated valleys in the Rockies, Minnesota's "2b's" are the coldest zones in the United States.

It's the length of summer, not the chill of winter, that matters to growers of annual plants like tomatoes and petunias. The statistic of interest here is the "growing season," which is measured as the number of days between the average date of the last 32° freeze in spring and the first freeze of fall. The shortest average growing season—88 days—is at Meadowlands, between Duluth and Hibbing, where early June and late August freezes are common. Here, one years in 10 may see a freeze as late as June 22 and as early as August 7, and July has even seen a 29° freeze! Donald Baker and Joseph Strub at the University of Minnesota Agricultural Experiment Station examined the Meadowlands climate, and concluded that the soil is to blame for the frosty summers. While Duluth and Hibbing lie on rocky ground, Meadowlands sits in a belt of organic soil. The light and relatively fluffy organic soil effectively insulates the air above from heat stored in the ground beneath, allowing the air to cool faster at night. Apparently, the nature of the soil trims a whopping 24 days from Meadlowlands' growing season!

Meadowlands' tomato growers might be advised to move south. Minnesota's longest growing seasons are found right along the Mississippi River in the extreme southeastern corner of the state. La Crosse airport, located on an island in the Mississippi, average 174 growing days. True, La Crosse and its airport are in Wisconsin, but it's representative of the area. Within the Twin Cities metropolitan area, growing seasons run from 162 to 167 days (longest at Minneapolis–St. Paul airport, not that anybody grows food there). Just beyond the fringes of the metroplex, the growing seasons at places like Chaska, Farmington, and Maple Plain are about two weeks shorter (144 to 151 days). Metropolitan gardeners can thank the "urban heat island" for their bigger zucchinis—heat given off by industries and

EXTREME MINIMUM AIR TEMPERATURE
Recorded during the total record period

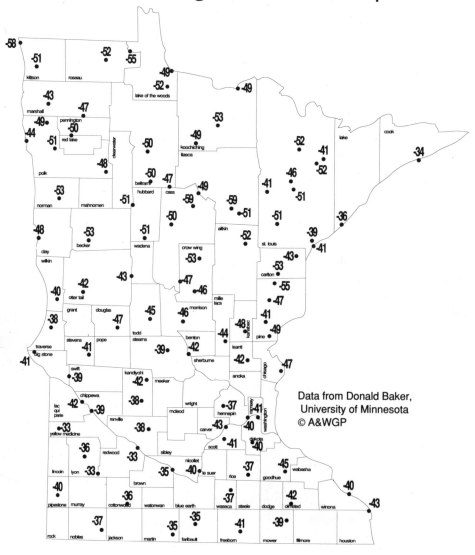

Data from Donald Baker,
University of Minnesota
© A&WGP

EXTREME MAXIMUM AIR TEMPERATURE
Recorded during the total record period

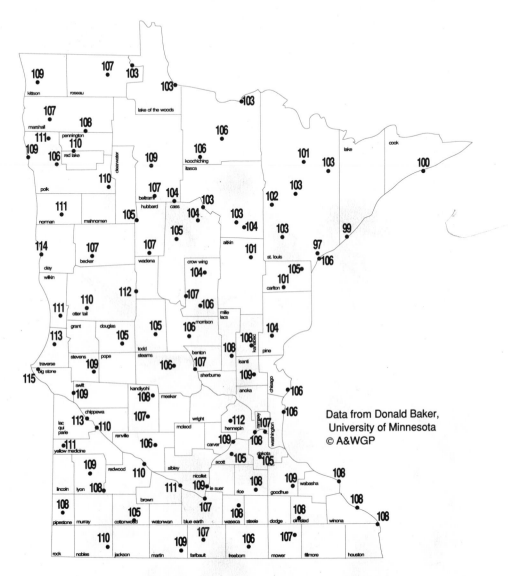

Data from Donald Baker,
University of Minnesota
© A&WGP

residences, combined with the previous afternoon's warmth stored in concrete and asphalt, can keep the city 5° to 10° warmer on the clear, calm nights typical of those late spring and early fall freezes.

We're not done with cold yet, either. It's not the averages that make the news. It's the extremes. The most extreme low ever recorded in Minnesota stands at 59° below zero, set at Leech Lake Dam on February 9, 1899, and at Pokegama Dam on February 16, 1903.

JANUARY NORMAL MINIMUM TEMPERATURES

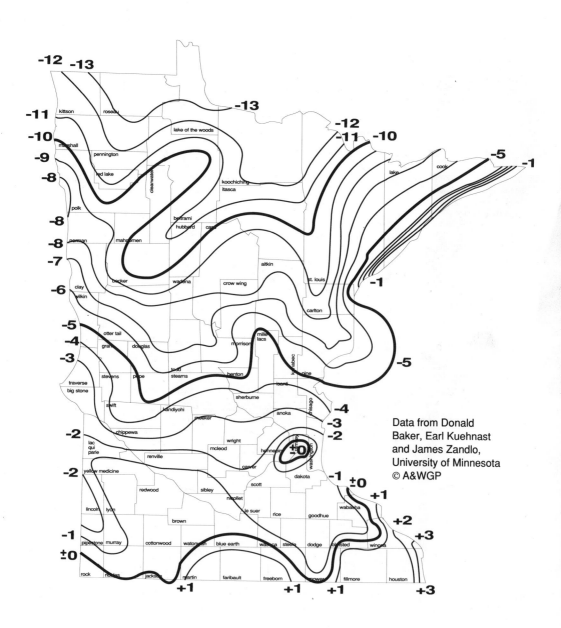

Data from Donald
Baker, Earl Kuehnast
and James Zandlo,
University of Minnesota
© A&WGP

JANUARY NORMAL MAXIMUM TEMPERATURES

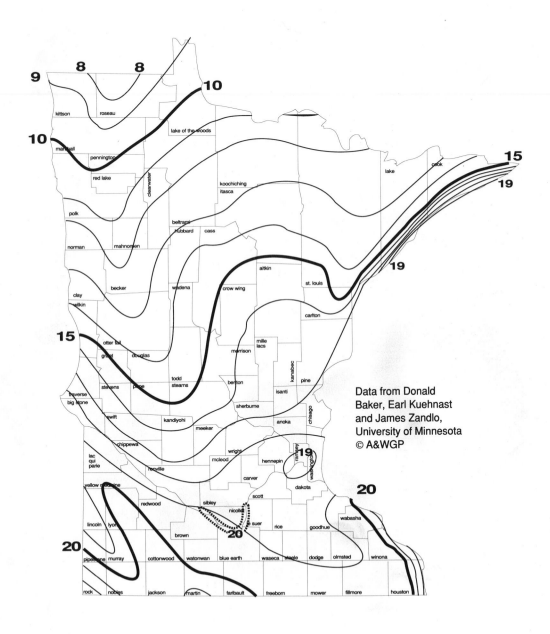

Data from Donald
Baker, Earl Kuehnast
and James Zandlo,
University of Minnesota
© A&WGP

Braving downtown Minneapolis during the ice storm of January 14, 1952.

However, the Pokegama Dam reading has come under suspicion, and Earl Kuehnast, former State Climatologist with the Minnesota Department of Natural Resources, has concluded that it is erroneous. The 1903 cold wave wasn't generally all that extreme, and Pokegama's 59° below was at least 17° lower than the temperature of any other nearby station. Furthermore, the observer's notes suggest that the thermometer was only a foot or so above the snow (standard height is 5 feet). At night, air cools from the ground (or snow surface) up, because the ground radiates its heat away to space, and the air cools by contact with the ground. Deep snow is an excellent heat radiator, and, like fiberglass batting, insulates the air from the relative warmth of the earth, and on clear, calm nights the snow surface may be 10° colder than the air at the normal 5-foot thermometer height.

But, the 1899 cold outbreak set records from Montana to Florida, and Leech Lake Dam's 59° below was surrounded by other readings in the 50° to 53° below zero range (Pokegama was only 50° below that time). In extreme northwestern Minnesota, St. Vincent was only 1 degree behind at 58° below. Thus, it appears the honors should go to Leech Lake Dam for recording Minnesota's lowest temperature, and to the February 1899 cold wave as the most intense in the state's history.

That was nearly a century ago, and some potentially cold spots that didn't have weather stations in 1899 have them now. In recent years the little hamlet of Embarrass, 64 miles due north of Duluth, has gained some fame as a cold spot. Low hills surround Embarrass on three side, with the fourth side being open to allow the Embarrass River to escape. Sitting in a little basin, the town is an ideal spot for low temperatures. At night, radiatively cooled air, being heavier than warm air, slides down the snow-covered hills and pools at the lowest point, namely, Embarrass. The town's a relatively new weather station, and its all-time low came in 1982, when the alcohol slipped to 52° below (mercury freezes at 40° below, so alcohol thermometers are used). Embarrass wasn't on the map in 1899, but perhaps another great arctic outbreak will come along someday, and a new champ will be found.

MORE LIKE AN OVEN

Let's warm up a bit, and check out the top of Minnesota's thermometer. In terms of annual temperature, the winner is—the envelope please—Winona! The annual average: 45.5°, a full 10° higher than that of Roseau. Nestled in the valley of the Mississippi at 652 feet above sea level, Winona is one of the lowest weather stations in the state—only Grand Marais and other spots along Lake Superior are lower. Its location in extreme southeastern Minnesota doesn't hurt, either. Compared to Roseau, Winona is 450 miles farther from the source of arctic cold waves, and its January average low—a pleasant 4° *above* zero, gives it the mildest winters in Minnesota. For the hottest summers, we must travel west to Canby, 150 miles west of the Twin Cities nine miles from South Dakota, where the average daily maximum temperature in July is 85.5°. The extreme southwestern corner of Minnesota may be a little warmer at 86°, according to a map published by the University of Minnesota's Agricultural Experiment Station, but without a long-term weather station there, that 86° is an estimate (not far away, Sioux Falls, South Dakota, averages 86.4°). Finally, the 63° aver-

JULY NORMAL MINIMUM TEMPERATURES

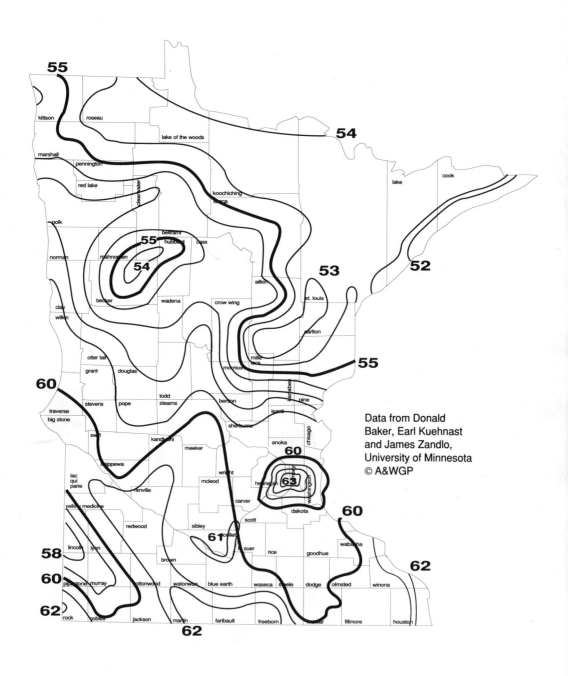

Data from Donald
Baker, Earl Kuehnast
and James Zandlo,
University of Minnesota
© A&WGP

JULY NORMAL MAXIMUM TEMPERATURES

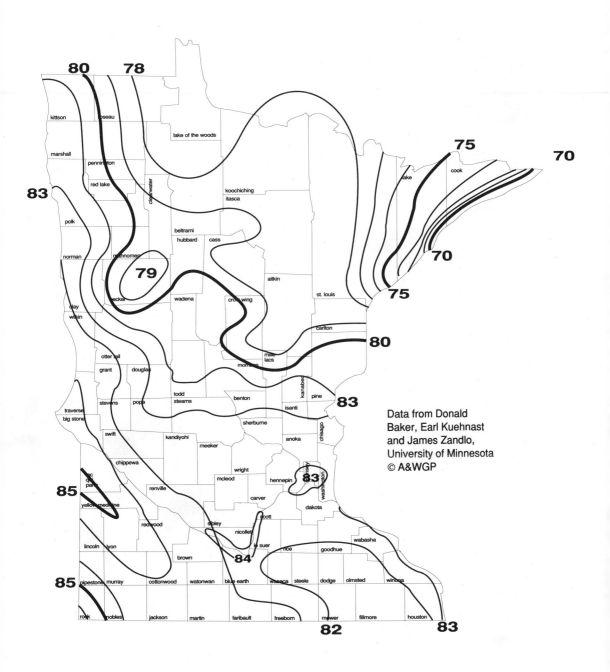

Data from Donald
Baker, Earl Kuehnast
and James Zandlo,
University of Minnesota
© A&WGP

age July daily minimum temperature at Minneapolis—St. Paul International Airport gives the Twin Cities the warmest summer nights in Minnesota (ah, the heat island!).

Those are the warmest averages; now for the hottest extremes. This one is almost, but not quite, a tie between Beardsley and Moorhead. Moorhead soared to 114° (113.9°, to be exact) on July 6, 1936, during the most protracted and intense heat wave ever known in Minnesota.

Sixteen states and two Canadian provinces, from Texas to Manitoba to New Jersey, set all-time highs that summer, making 1936 the heat wave equivalent of the great 1899 cold wave. In North Dakota, Steele (just east of Bismarck) soared to 121°, a state record exceeded only by those of deserts in Arizona, California and Nevada. In July 1936, Minneapolis, Rochester and St. Cloud all set their all-time high temperature records. Duluth's downtown temperature reached 106°, while the Coast Guard registered 108° at the harbor entrance. Back at Moorhead, the Moorhead *Daily News* reported on that scorching 6th of July that "a group of gentlemen sat about an entrance-way of the city hall at 3 p.m. watching an egg fry on the pavement." Eggs need at least 125° to cook, and they cook faster if it's hotter; the August sun could have heated the concrete as high as 140°.

The paper didn't report how long it took to fry that egg, but one probably would have cooked a little faster in Beardsley on July 29, 1917. It was a strange year. At Duluth, Minneapolis and St. Paul, and for a statewide average, 1917 was the coldest year in the past century. Duluth had its coldest June and shortest frost-free season ever. Even at Beardsley, which sits near the tip of Minnesota's little bulge into South Dakota, the summer got off to a chilly start. The observer, J. Fitzgerald, recorded "frost in spots" on July 2 and 3. On the 11th he noted, simply, a "tornado"!

Hundred-degree heat struck Beardsley on the 21st, but for the next week, while Beardsley simmered, the rest of the state remained comfortable. On the 28th the reluctant heat wave intensified and swept east, raising thermometers to the century mark across the state. At Beardsley the mercury touched 113° during "a very hot wind." The next day's reading was 114.5° ; let's call it 115°, Minnesota's all-time high. Mr. Fitzgerald commented that winds were "almost calm," but said nothing about frying eggs. Beardsley's high is often reported as 114°, a tie with Moorhead; however, that extra half-degree actually rounds up to 115°—and Beardsley wins the title. Half a degree might not sound like much, but, like a single hit in the 10th inning of the 7th game of the World Series, it can make the difference between first and next place!

Only about one sixth of Minnesota's towns have seen temperatures as high as 110°, and the majority of these are strung along the Red and Minnesota rivers from Moorhead to New Ulm. This 250-mile-long stretch of river land owes its warmth to something most Minnesotans wouldn't consider an important factor in their climate: altitude. Minnesota is pretty flat, thanks to those mile-deep glaciers of the Ice Age. All of Minnesota lies between 602' (along Lake Superior) and 2,301' (eagle Mountain, in Cook County) above sea level, an elevation range of 1,699'. Of the 50 states, only 12 have a lesser spread between their highest and lowest points.

The highest elevations in southwestern Minnesota are along the Buffalo Ridge, also known as Coteau des Prairies (Little Plateau of the Prairie), which rises to near 2,000' north of Pipestone and extends northwest into South Dakota. From the Buffalo Ridge the ground drops to the northeast, bottoming out 50 miles away at elevations below 1,000' along the Minnesota and Red rivers. Breezes from the southwest (the favored direction on hot days) cross the ridge and then blow downhill. As the air loses altitude, it heats by compression

A Twin Cities' rotary snow plow attacks snow from the 1940 Armistice Day blizzard.

at the rate of 5.5° per 1,000'. That's enough to warm things up by 5° or 6°, making hot days hotter and some winter days much more pleasant. It's Minnesota's version of the "chinook" winds that toast the valleys of the Rockies, and is the reason places like Beardsley, Milan, Moorhead, and Wheaton can boast of being Minnesota's Oven—or, as was demonstrated in Moorhead—Frying Pan!

BUT IT FEELS LIKE...

It should go without saying that all those numbers you have just read are straight temperatures, recorded right off a thermometer. Lately a variety of heat and cold indices have been reported on weather broadcasts and in newspapers. While they are reported in degrees and sound like temperatures, indices are definitely not temperatures. Indeed, these numbers purportedly give a better measure of how much cold or heat we *feel* when we're outside.

The most familiar of these indices is the "wind chill." The original formula for wind chill factors was developed by Paul Siple, who spent the winter of 1941 at Little America,

Antarctica, setting pints of warm water outside and watching them freeze. From the time taken for the pints to freeze in various weather conditions, Siple derived "heat-loss" rates for different combinations of wind speed and temperature. Originally, the heat-loss rates were expressed in kilogram-calories per square meter per hour, but this proved difficult for television weathercasters to say in their five-minute time slots. So the idea came up to express the heat loss as an "equivalent temperature." For example, a pint set out on a 5° day with a 45-mile-per-hour wind froze as quickly as one set out at 45° below with a 4 m.p.h. wind. The 4 m.p.h. wind speed was chosen for comparison because people are rarely stationary when they're outside in cold weather. Usually folks walk briskly, or at least mill smartly, when it's below freezing, giving an effective wind speed of about 4 m.p.h. (the speed of a brisk walk) even when the wind is calm.

Wind chill factors can get quite impressive. On two Saturdays in a row, January 9 and 16, 1982, temperatures below -30° and winds above 40 m.p.h. produced wind chills in excess of 100° below zero across most of northern Minnesota! In general, wind chills below -35° present a real danger of frostbite, prompting the National Weather Service to issue "Wind Chill Advisories."

In Russia, where it *really* gets cold, researchers have examined the effect of wind chills in some detail. They taped tiny thermometers on the ears, noses and cheeks of volunteers who strolled about in the Siberian cold, and measured the skin temperature after various time intervals. The result was an equation that gives the "face temperature" after 30 minutes outside, and, like the wind chill factor, depends on air temperature and wind speed. Under calm conditions, a 40° below zero air temperature will chill an average face to 32° in 30 minutes, raising the threat of frostbite (ears chill faster than the rest of the face, and will be down to 25° by this point). With 100°-below-zero wind chills like those recorded in Northern Minnesota in January 1982, face temperatures will drop to 9° (ears, 2°) in half an hour—obviously, a serious situation. Presumably, the Russian researchers brought their volunteers inside long before their face temperatures reached 9°!

When it's 80°, and the wind is still blowing at 40 m.p.h., the wind chill factor computes to be 75°. However, when it's that warm nobody really cares about wind chills anymore, and the whole idea becomes meaningless when the air becomes as warm as your skin (about 91°). During the summer, as they say, "it's not the heat, it's the humidity" that determines outdoor comfort (or discomfort). Actually, it's both heat *and* humidity that come into play. On hot days, skin moisture (sweat) evaporates into the air to cool the body to a comfortable temperature. The lower the humidity, the more rapid the evaporation, and the cooler we feel. On the other hand, with a humidity of 100 percent there is little or no evaporation, and we feel quite muggy. Early heat indices, like the "Temperature-Humidity Index" (or, THI) used in the 1960s, reflected the evaporative cooling effect of low humidities by always reading lower than the actual air temperature. So, on a dry 100° day the THI might read 80°. However, folks like to think of humidity as making it feel warmer, rather than dryness making it seem cooler, so the THI never really caught on.

Now the National Weather Service routinely issues "Apparent Temperatures," or simply

WIND CHILL AND HEAT INDEX TABLES

These tables list wind chills and heat indices for various combinations of actual temperature and wind speed (or relative humidity). They're fairly self-explanatory, but here are a couple of examples: When it's 0° with a 10 m.p.h. wind, 20° with a 45 m.p.h. wind, or 22° below with no wind, the wind chill is -22°. Six months later, if it's 85° and the humidity reads 60 percent, the apparent temperature is 90°, but if the humidity is only 20 percent, the apparent temperature is 82°. Asterisks (*) indicate combinations of temperature and humidity that are extremely unlikely (nothing's impossible, though) in Minnesota.

WIND CHILL INDEX

ACTUAL TEMPERATURE

WIND SPEED (M.P.H.)	40	30	20	10	0	-10	-20	-30	-40	-50
0-4	40	30	20	10	0	-10	-20	-30	-40	-50
5	37	27	16	6	-5	-15	-26	-36	-47	-57
10	28	16	3	-9	-22	-34	-46	-58	-71	-83
15	23	9	-5	-18	-31	-45	-58	-72	-85	-99
20	19	4	-10	-24	-39	-53	-67	-81	-95	-110
25	16	1	-15	-29	-44	-59	-74	-88	-103	-117
30	13	-2	-18	-33	-49	-64	-79	-93	-109	-123
35	12	-4	-20	-35	-52	-67	-82	-97	-113	-128
40	11	-5	-21	-37	-53	-69	-84	-100	-115	-131
45	10	-6	-22	-38	-54	-70	-85	-102	-117	-133

HEAT INDEX (APPARENT TEMPERATURE)

ACTUAL TEMPERATURE

RELATIVE HUMIDITY	70	75	80	85	90	95	100	105	110	115
0	64*	69*	73*	78*	83*	87*	91*	95*	99*	103*
10	65	70	75	80	85	90	95	100	105	111
20	66	72	77	82	87	93	99	105	112	120
30	67	73	78	84	90	96	104	113	123	135*
40	68	74	79	86	93	101	110	123	137*	151*
50	69	75	81	88	96	107	120	135*	150*	
60	70	76	83	90	100	114	132*	149*		
70	70	77	85	93	106	124*	144*			
80	71	78	87	97	113*	136*				
90	71	79	89	102*	122*					
100	72	80	91	108*						

the "Heat Index," which relate temperature and humidity combinations to equivalent temperatures at low humidities. The index is based on years of physiological studies, and includes such factors as the person's size, weight, metabolism, clothing, amount of sweating, and body temperature, along with wind, sunshine, and, of course, air temperature and humidity. To simplify matters, the Heat Index is computed for a 5-foot 7-inch, 147-pound person wearing long trousers and a short-sleeved shirt covering 84 percent of the body, with no sunshine and a 5 m.p.h. wind, et cetera, leaving only temperature and humidity to determine the index. With a 35 percent humidity at 105° (fairly extreme for Minnesota), the Apparent Temperature works out 118°, the same index as 130° at 1 percent humidity, or 118° and 14 percent humidity. A more likely heat wave with 95° and 50 percent humidity "feels like" 107° at 17 percent humidity. Note that, unlike the wind chill's standard of 4 m.p.h. wind speed, the reference low humidity is not constant.

So, what use is this "Apparent Temperature"? For one, it helps the National Weather Service decide when conditions warrant issuing "heat stress" warnings for people and livestock. At an apparent temperature of 105°, for example, some people may suffer sunstroke or heat exhaustion if they don't take it easy, and a few may undergo heat stroke (a potentially fatal condition). Predicted indices give power companies an idea of how much current will go into air conditioners that day. But apparent temperatures are also a "gee whiz" thing, just like the wind chill, giving folks an opportunity to say "it felt like a hundred and eighteen," which sounds more impressive than saying "it was a hundred and five."

Neither the wind chill or the heat index is a temperature. They may *look* like temperatures, since they're given in degrees, but temperatures are what you read off a thermometer—no more and no less. Unfortunately, while these indices provide realistic measures of what the outdoors may feel like, they have been used so much that they are often confused with temperature. Actually, one of these indices is more likely to make its way into a newspaper than the actual temperature. The result is that I've heard people say that "we had eighty below last winter!" believing that the temperature, not the wind chill, was really 80° below! The whole idea behind wind chills and heat indices is to improve on simple temperature as an indicator of what it's like outside. Once the indices become confused with actual temperatures, their purpose has been totally defeated. Perhaps they should be used a bit more sparingly.

MINNESOTA WEATHER EXTREMES AND RECORDS

■■■■■■■■■■■■■■■■■■■■■■■■■■■■

Minnesota has its share of weather extremes. Here are some of them.

Geography

Highest place: Eagle Mountain (Cook County), 2,301 feet above sea level.

Lowest place: Along Lake Superior, 602 feet (the highest and lowest places are only 12 miles apart).

Temperature (averages based on 1951-1980)

Warmest place: Winona, 45.5° annual average temperature.

Coldest place: Roseau, 35.3° annual average temperature.

Hottest summer days: Canby, average July maximum 85.5°.

Coldest winter nights: Roseau, average January daily minimum -12.4°.

Hottest ever: 114.5° at Beardsley, July 29, 1917.

Coldest ever: -59° at Leech Lake Dam, February 9, 1899, and at Pokegama Dam, February 16, 1903 (the latter reading is suspect).

Warmest month: 83.4° at Pipestone, July 1936.

Coldest month: -14.4° at Hallock, February 1936.

Warmest year, state-wide average: 1931, annual average 45.9°.

Coldest year, state-wide average: 1917, annual average 36.5°.

Longest heat wave (daily maximum over 100°): 13 days, Beardsley and Zumbrota, July 6-18, 1936.

Longest cold wave (daily maximum below zero): 19 days, Breckenridge, January 2-20, 1875.

Warmest night: 87° overnight low, June 30, 1931, at Canby.

Coldest day: -39° afternoon maximum, Feb. 8, 1899, at Roseau.

Longest growing season: 174 days (April 25 to October 16) on the border at La Crosse, Wisconsin. (Growing seasons are measured from the average date of the last 32° temperature in spring to the first freeze in fall.)

Shortest growing season: 88 days (June 4 to August 31) at Meadowlands.

Precipitation

Wettest place: Caledonia, 34.25" average annual precipitation.

Driest place: Argyle, 19.01" average annual precipitation.

Most precipitation in one year: 51.53" at Grand Meadow, 1911.

Least precipitation in one year: 7.81" at Angus, 1936.

Wettest year, state-wide: 1977, 33.92" precipitation.

Driest year, state-wide: 1910, 14.65" precipitation.

Most rain in 24 hours: 14.00" in Parker Township, July 21-22, 1972.

Greatest downpour (unofficial): 30" to 36" in as many hours at Sauk Centre and Osakis, July 18, 1867.

Snow

Snowiest place: Pigeon River, averaged 107.4" snow per year, 1931-1950.

Least snowy place: Angus, averaged 27.0" snow per year, 1904-60.

Most snow in one winter: 147.5" at Pigeon River, 1936-37.

Least snow in one winter: 2.3" at Austin, 1967-68.

Most snow in one month: 66.4" at Collegeville, March 1965.

Most snow in a single storm: 36.9" at Duluth, Oct. 31-Nov. 3, 1991.

Barometric Pressure (reduced to sea level):

Highest: 31.11" at Collegeville, Jan. 21, 1922.

Lowest: 28.57" at Duluth, Jan. 11, 1975. The pressure in this storm fell to an estimated 28.40" as it passed west of Grand Portage. Even lower pressures have undoubtedly occurred in tornadoes.

Wind

Fastest measured speed: 110 m.p.h. (1-minute average) at St. Paul during the tornado of August 20, 1904.

Tornadoes

First recorded: April 18, 1820, at Fort Snelling.

Deadliest: 74 killed at Sauk Rapids–St. Cloud, April 14, 1886.

Most in one year: 34 in 1968.

Most damaging outbreak: $57 million on May 6, 1965, as six tornadoes struck the northern and western portions of the Twin Cities metropolitan area.

Hail

Largest stone: 12" circumference near Detroit Lakes, July 4, 1966.

Largest stone (unofficial): 16" circumference near Claremont, Dodge County, October 14, 1966.

Heaviest stone (unofficial): 5 pounds at John Holper farm, July 27, 1910.

Disasters

Most lives lost: 1,000 (estimated) in Pine and Carlton county fires, October 12, 1918.

Greatest damage: $273 million in the Red River floods, June-July, 1975.

MINNESOTA WEATHER EXTREMES

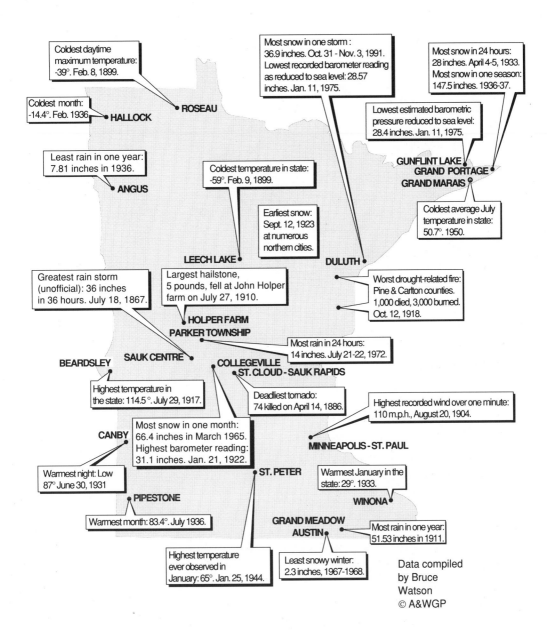

Coldest daytime maximum temperature: -39°. Feb. 8, 1899.

Coldest month: -14.4°. Feb. 1936.

HALLOCK

ROSEAU

Most snow in one storm : 36.9 inches. Oct. 31 - Nov. 3, 1991. Lowest recorded barometer reading as reduced to sea level: 28.57 inches. Jan. 11, 1975.

Most snow in 24 hours: 28 inches. April 4-5, 1933. Most snow in one season: 147.5 inches. 1936-37.

Least rain in one year: 7.81 inches in 1936.

ANGUS

Lowest estimated barometric pressure reduced to sea level: 28.4 inches. Jan. 11, 1975.

GUNFLINT LAKE
GRAND PORTAGE
GRAND MARAIS

Coldest temperature in state: -59°. Feb. 9, 1899.

Earliest snow: Sept. 12, 1923 at numerous northern cities.

Coldest average July temperature in state: 50.7°. 1950.

LEECH LAKE

DULUTH

Greatest rain storm (unofficial): 36 inches in 36 hours. July 18, 1867.

Largest hailstone, 5 pounds, fell at John Holper farm on July 27, 1910.

Worst drought-related fire: Pine & Carlton counties. 1,000 died, 3,000 burned. Oct. 12, 1918.

HOLPER FARM
PARKER TOWNSHIP

Most rain in 24 hours: 14 inches. July 21-22, 1972.

BEARDSLEY   **SAUK CENTRE**   **COLLEGEVILLE**
ST. CLOUD - SAUK RAPIDS

Highest temperature in the state: 114.5°. July 29, 1917.

Deadliest tornado: 74 killed on April 14, 1886.

Highest recorded wind over one minute: 110 m.p.h., August 20, 1904.

Most snow in one month: 66.4 inches in March 1965. Highest barometer reading: 31.1 inches. Jan. 21, 1922.

CANBY

MINNEAPOLIS - ST. PAUL

Warmest night: Low 87° June 30, 1931

ST. PETER

Warmest January in the state: 29°. 1933.

PIPESTONE

WINONA

Warmest month: 83.4°. July 1936.

GRAND MEADOW
AUSTIN

Most rain in one year: 51.53 inches in 1911.

Highest temperature ever observed in January: 65°. Jan. 25, 1944.

Least snowy winter: 2.3 inches, 1967-1968.

Data compiled by Bruce Watson
© A&WGP

31

SOLID STATE: ICE AND SNOW

■ ■

ICE WATCHER'S PARADISE

It's hard to imagine what life would be like without ice. Without ice, what would there be skate on? How could you walk out onto a lake to go fishing? There would be nothing to shovel in the winter, and no reason to change tires twice a year. No "frost on the pumpkin," and nothing to collapse the inflatable roofs of sports arenas. And what would beat crops to a pulp in June? For better or worse, ice is part of life in Minnesota. Ice is frozen water. That seems simple enough, but ice is far from simple. There are dozens of ways and dozens of places water can freeze into ice. The resulting ice crystals can take on any of hundreds of forms, and Minnesotans see them all (well, almost all)!

Perhaps the most familiar thing about ice crystals is their distinctive six-sided, or hexagonal, shape (salt crystals, on the other hand, are little cubes). We see this hexagonal pattern in snowflakes and frost, on icy window panes, or anywhere else ice has formed (if you look closely enough). Water is a molecule consisting of two hydrogen atoms attached to a single, larger oxygen atom. The angle between the hydrogen atoms is 120°, the same angle as the "corners" of a hexagon. So, when water molecules bind together to form solid ice, this 120° angle appears throughout the entire mass of ice, accounting for the characteristic six-sided structure of ice crystals.

Ice can form in all sorts of places in all sorts of ways. Ice produced in the atmosphere may fall as snow or hail to the ground, or stay in the sky as ice crystal clouds. Ice also can form directly on the ground or on the surfaces of lakes, streams, and ponds. The freezing of liquid water makes ice, but ice can also "sublimate" directly from individual molecules of water vapor (a gas). Ice formed by sublimation usually grows into large, well-defined crystals, while crystals in ice frozen from liquid water may be so small that the ice appears amorphous. The result of sublimation, "hoar frost," is what decorates windows. Organic impurities on window surfaces interfere with natural crystal growth and can cause curved shapes.

It may seem obvious that ice requires only two conditions: the presence of water and below-freezing temperatures. However, some varieties of ice, notably frost and "black ice" on highways, can form when the air temperature is slightly above freezing but the ground has cooled by radiation to below the freezing point. Evaporation can chill wet objects below the freezing point, even though the air is warmer than freezing. That's how you can get frozen laundry on a 35° day. On the other hand, water doesn't always freeze as soon as the temperature drops to 32°. Undisturbed pure water can remain liquid at temperatures as low as 40° below zero; this "supercooled" water is observed in clouds. Outside of clouds, most water contains enough impurities and is disturbed enough (by such things as breezes rippling the surface) to freeze right at 32°. Perhaps you've heard stories about ducks landing in supercooled ponds only to have the water freeze solid around their feet. That's a great example of supercooled water in action; however, I've never seen evidence that this duck's tale has actually ever happened!

Minnesota is an ice watcher's paradise. Although ice is much cheaper than diamonds, it can be every bit as beautiful and displays a lot more variety. The obvious place for Minnesotans to see ice is, of course, a lake. The incredible diversity of ever-changing frozen forms seen on lakes is enough to keep the pickiest ice-watcher enthralled, but even more interesting—and important—is the freeze-up and thaw cycle of the lake itself. The freezing of a lake is not just a bigger version of an ice cube tray in a freezer, and the reason involves some unusual properties of water.

ANNUAL LAKE FREEZE CYCLE

Water is strange stuff. First of all, very few substances are liquid at what we consider "normal" temperatures and atmospheric pressures. Water, fortunately, is one of them. Furthermore, water happens to solidify (freeze) at a commonly occurring temperature—not like mercury, which freezes at 40° below, or iron, which "freezes" at 2,786° Fahrenheit. So, we get to see water in both its liquid and solid states without suffering too much.

Even stranger, though, is what water does when it freezes—it expands! Most substances shrink when they solidify. One pound of ice takes up 10 percent more volume than one pound of liquid water, so 10 gallons of water make 11 gallons of ice. That explains the bulges that grow in the middle of ice cubes. Looking at it another way, one gallon of water weighs about 8 pounds, but one gallon of ice weights 10 percent *less,* or just over 7 pounds. That's why ice cubes float in water.

The third (and final) odd property of water is what happens to it at temperatures just above freezing. Almost every known material expands when it is heated, and contracts when cooled. Water is fairly normal in that regard most of the time. As a cup of liquid water cools from its boiling point of 212°, it shrinks and becomes denser (same volume weighs more). It keeps shrinking all the way down to 39°, but then further cooling actually causes the cup of water to expand a little. This means that 39° water is denser than water at any other temperature (higher or lower), and that water at any other temperature will "float" in a layer on top of the 39° water.

That fact that water is a liquid is clearly significant for Earth's living things. However, the other two properties of water—that ice floats and 33° water is "lighter" than 39° water—may seem like mere curiosities. However, if water were more normal, and ice didn't float, and 33° water wasn't "lighter" than 39° water, Minnesota's lakes—and the world's oceans—would be very, very different, and quite unpleasant, places. Let me explain...

We'll start in the fall, when increasingly chilly air removes the summer warmth from the surface of a medium-size lake (say, Minnetonka). The air also removes moisture from the lake (by evaporation), and if the lake is still warm enough and the air cool enough, you can see this moisture rising from the lake as streamers of steam. The cooling effect is first felt at the lake surface, where the autumn breezes directly remove heat from the water molecules. This cools a very thin layer at the top of a, say, 50° lake to 49°, making the surface layer denser (or "heavier") than the rest of the lake. The surface water sinks in little downward plumes, eventually mixing with the rest of the lake, and the whole lake cools a fraction of a degree.

By early November the whole lake has cooled to 39°. Now when the surface layer cools further—to 38°—it is no longer denser than the deeper water, and it stays floating on top. The more it cools the "lighter" it gets, and by late November the top layer of the lake is 32°, but still liquid, while the deeper lake water remains at 39°. The depth of the cold surface layer depends on the amount of churning by wind and waves, and big lakes (like Superior) with big waves have deeper layers than do small lakes and ponds. Shortly after the top of the lake reaches 32°, the first ice forms. Only the surface layer (and not the entire depth of the lake) has cooled below 39°, so thanks to one of the peculiar properties of water, the first ice freezes several weeks sooner than it would otherwise.

On ponds the first ice forms in clear, smooth, glass-like sheets that grow out from rocks and reeds. As the ice crystals reach out toward the center of the lake, additional ice freezes to the bottom of the glassy sheet. Tiny bubbles of trapped air give the thickening ice a milky white appearance. The ice becomes safe for walking and ice skating when it's 4" thick, and cars can be driven on clear, solid ice that's at least 8" thick.

Waves on larger lakes (like Superior) break up the first ice into a slushy surface layer floating crystals, sometimes called "grease" or "frazil" ice. These crystals stick together and grow into small floes of "pancake" ice. If the weather stays cold long enough, the floes freeze together into a solid sheet of "pack" ice, which may eventually cover the entire lake or stay confined to near-shore areas. Wind and currents can push pieces of pack ice apart, opening up large cracks or "leads," which may close up again as the wind changes direction. When pack ice is pushed against the shore or other chunks of pack ice, the frozen layer can buckle and crumble into jagged "pressure ridges," the bane of arctic explorers but fun to look at.

Because of its enormous volume, Lake Superior usually doesn't develop substantial ice cover until late January (although bays and inlets may freeze in November). And unlike every other lake in Minnesota, Superior rarely freezes over completely. In an average winter 40 percent of the lake (mostly near the middle of the lake) remains ice-free, with ice packs either sticking to shore or wandering about with the changing winds. With open water at mid-winter, spray may coat ships and shoreline structures with massive loads of ice during bouts of cold and windy weather, while along the shoreline massive walls of ice, grounded to the beach, are built up by continuous rains of freezing spray.

At long last, spring arrives. Warm winds and increasing sunshine heat the top of the ice while the relative warmth of the underlying 39° water works its way up, and the ice thins from both sides. Around the first week of April along the Iowa border, mid-April for the Twin Cities, and by early May in the far north, the ice breaks up and disappears from most lakes. Lake Superior's ice pack shows signs of decay around the first of April, on the average, but the enormous mass of ice that has accumulated during the winter usually doesn't disappear until May, and has on occasion (as in 1972) lingered into June or (in 1876) July.

With the ice gone, summer approaching, and the sun riding higher in the sky, lake surfaces warm rapidly. When the surface temperature reaches 39°, surface water has the same density as the deep water. After being confined to the deeper reaches since fall, the

TYPES OF SNOW CRYSTALS

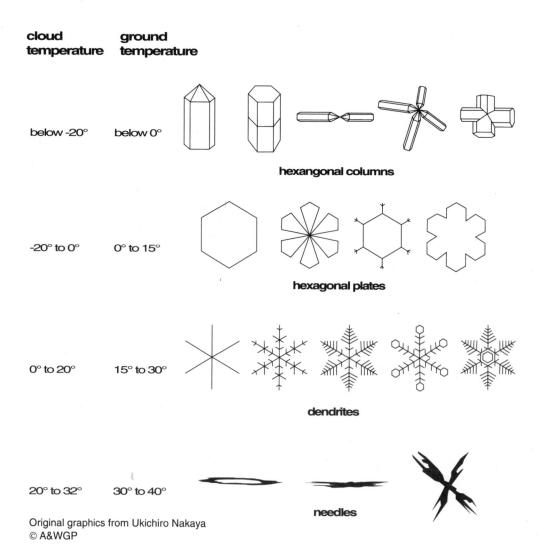

cloud temperature **ground temperature**

below -20°   below 0°

hexangonal columns

-20° to 0°   0° to 15°

hexagonal plates

0° to 20°   15° to 30°

dendrites

20° to 32°   30° to 40°

needles

Original graphics from Ukichiro Nakaya
© A&WGP

39° bottom water is finally able to rise to the surface—bringing with it all sorts of goodies, like dead fish, that have sat on the bottom for six months. In return, oxygen-rich surface water sinks to the bottom. This turn-over period can be a smelly time, but it doesn't last long. Once the surface warms above 40° it is once again "lighter" than the deeper water.

The warming continues until late July or early August, by which time the lowering sun angle becomes ineffective at heating the lake any further. Peak water temperatures depend on the location, and more importantly the size, of the lake. Medium-sized lakes in southern Minnesota, like Minnetonka, may reach 80° in mid-summer, about the same temperature as the Pacific Ocean around Hawaii! On the other hand, Lake Superior normally gets no warmer than 53°, and usually not until late August (bays and near-shore waters may get a bit warmer, though). In all lakes, the surface warms more than the deep water. On a still summer day the warm surface layer may be only one or two feet deep, something not unnoticed by swimmers. Sunlight penetrates 100 feet or so into clear water, so most lakes' deep water warms up during the summer, although it never gets quite as warm as the surface. The exception is, of course, Lake Superior. Superior is the deepest of the Great Lakes, with most of the lake deeper than 300 feet and as deep as 1,290 feet deep at one point. At these depths the water never knows summer has come or gone, and the temperature remains 39° year-round. By September all the lakes have started cooling down for another icy winter.

Now, just for the fun of it, consider what would happen if ice did *not* float. As soon as it formed, ice would sink to the bottoms of rivers, lakes, and oceans. Ice, and snow lying atop it, are great heat insulators—that is, they block the transfer of heat from one side to the other. Once lakes freeze over and the ice thickens, the rate of new ice formation slows down considerably. Without the insulating effect of floating ice sheets, surface waters would continue to rapidly lose heat and the ice continue to form (and sink). Eventually, large bodies of water such as the Arctic Ocean and Hudson's Bay, and perhaps even Lake Superior, might freeze solid as the ice accumulated from the bottom up. Since sunlight heats only the uppermost 100 feet (and the topmost few feet most effectively), summer thaws would be confined to thin surface layers that would quickly refreeze the following winter. Smaller and shallower lakes would still thaw completely every summer, although it might take until June or July. Lake Superior might never thaw out, to the consternation of not only Duluthians. The presence of a frozen Lake Superior, along with Hudson's Bay and Arctic Ocean, would have a tremendous chilling effect on the climate of all of Minnesota, particularly during the summer. But this is all speculation, because, fortunately, ice does float.

SNOW, AND OTHER ICE FROM THE SKY

Ice forms in the sky, and falls to earth, as snow, sleet, hail, and several other varieties of frozen precipitation. Of these, the most basic and most common is snow. Virtually all of the precipitation, be it liquid or frozen, that falls on Minnesota initially developed as snow. Yes, even a torrential downpour on a steamy 95° August day started out as snow.

Snowflakes are born when atmospheric moisture condenses onto small particles of dust, smoke, pollen, or other airborne stuff. Most snowflakes get their moisture from supercooled water droplets in clouds, but when it's *really* cold small ice crystals grow directly from sublimation of water vapor, without any clouds present. Sometimes—even in the summer—snow can be seen falling from high clouds and evaporating long before reaching the ground. When the snow melts before touching down, it's called "rain"!

The structure and size of ice crystals depend on the temperature and moisture content of the air in which they form. Crystals that grow from the meager water supply at 20° below zero or colder form pencil-shaped "hexagonal columns." Around zero to 10 below most crystals are flat, six-sided "hexagonal plates." Warmer air contains more moisture, allowing larger crystals to grow. At zero to 20° above, crystals grow into large and delicate six-pointed "dendrites," named from the Greek word meaning "branched like a tree." Dendrites are the largest form of snowflakes and make the fluffiest snowfalls. Between 20° and 32°, crystals grow into splinter-shaped "needles." Temperatures near the ground are typically 15° or 20° higher than the temperatures at cloud height, so light, fluffy falls of dendrites are usually seen at surface temperatures in the 15° to 30° range. With all their branches, dendrites have no problem sticking to each other and creating large, multi-crystal "aggregates" as large as 2" or 3" across.

Winds above 20 m.p.h. can return fallen snow to the air, creating drifting and blowing snow. By definition, drifting snow remains within five feet of the snow surface, and while it does not strongly affect visibility at eye level, it can impede motor traffic by depositing snow on highways faster than plows can remove it. Blowing snow is raised more than five feet above the ground, usually requiring winds in excess of 35 m.p.h. A snow storm is a "blizzard" when heavy falling snow combines with blowing snow and winds of 35 m.p.h. or higher to reduce visibilities to near zero; the official weather service definition also requires temperatures of 20° or less. "Ground blizzards" with heavy blowing snow and strong winds may continue for hours or days after the falling snow has stopped. Drifts and pits of scoured and deposited wind-blown snow are known by their Russian name, "sastrugi." Strong winds may even catch the edge of a wet and sticky snow layer, rolling it up like sleeping bags into "snow rollers"—a unique and rarely seen phenomenon!

We already mentioned that most of Minnesota's rain is snow that has melted while falling through above-freezing air near the ground. Sometimes from late autumn through early spring a below-freezing layer of arctic air hugs the ground while milder air streams in aloft (usually on the northeast side of an approaching cyclone). Then the snow that melts in the mild air refreezes before striking the ground. These re-frozen rain drops are "sleet" or, officially, "ice pellets." When the cold air layer is shallower than 1,000 feet or so, the raindrops cool down but don't freeze until they land on cold trees, roads, wires, and grass. Meteorologists call this "freezing rain" (of course!) or "glaze"; the rest of us know the result as an "ice storm." (Not to be confused with "rime" ice, which forms when supercooled droplets of *fog* freeze onto exposed surfaces.) While ice storms bestow the beauty of fine crystal on all they touch, the sad truth is that whatever they touch suffers a loss in value!

Another way to re-freeze raindrops is send them back up to where the air is normally

ANNUAL 1951-1980 NORMAL SNOWFALL
(values in inches)

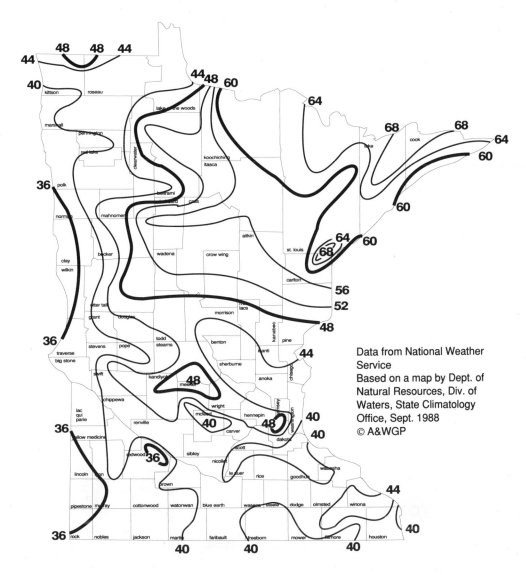

Data from National Weather
Service
Based on a map by Dept. of
Natural Resources, Div. of
Waters, State Climatology
Office, Sept. 1988
© A&WGP

colder. Rain that blows back up into a storm cloud, freezes and falls is also sleet, and looks identical to the sleet that freezes near the ground. Before reaching the ground, a sleet pellet might catch another updraft. On its way up through the cloud it collects some additional moisture, which freezes in a layer around the original tiny pellet. Depending on its luck, the growing pellet may make several trips up and down in the storm cloud, growing each time. Eventually the pellet escapes its updraft, or grows so large and heavy that the wind can't keep it up, and falls to earth as hail. Cut a hailstone open and you might see several layers of clear and white ice accumulated in different parts of the storm cloud, one layer for each trip through the cloud. The size of the hailstone tells something about the intensity of the storm. A baseball-size hailstone falls as fast as a major-league fastball, or about 90 m.p.h. That means that the updrafts must have been at least 90 m.p.h. for a stone that big to ascend inside the cloud. Updrafts that strong can easily become violent, and many large hailstorms also spawn tornadoes. Think about the power of the storm that dropped a five-pounder on Todd County in 1910!

Falling ice may take other forms, such as soft, white "snow pellets" or "graupel," which are a cross between snow and hail, tiny "snow grains" that fall from shallow cloud layers, and "diamond dust," tiny crystals that fall from clear skies when the temperature is below zero. However, snow, rain, sleet, glaze, and hail are the ones that fill the lakes and rivers, cause traffic accidents, give skiers and snowmobilers something to do, and nourish and destroy crops.

HOW MUCH & HOW OFTEN

Minnesota is a big state, and some places get more snow, or hail, or whatever, than other places do. As one might expect, annual snowfall is greater over northern Minnesota than it is in the south. Virtually all of the southern half of the state receives between 3' and 4'

MINNEAPOLIS SEASONAL SNOWFALL TOTALS, 1859-1990

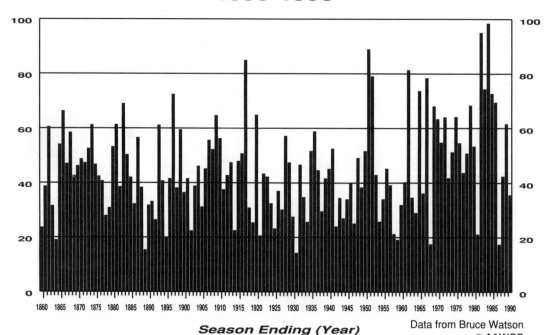

Season Ending (Year)

Data from Bruce Watson
© A&WGP

LAST FROST
All dates May unless otherwise indicated

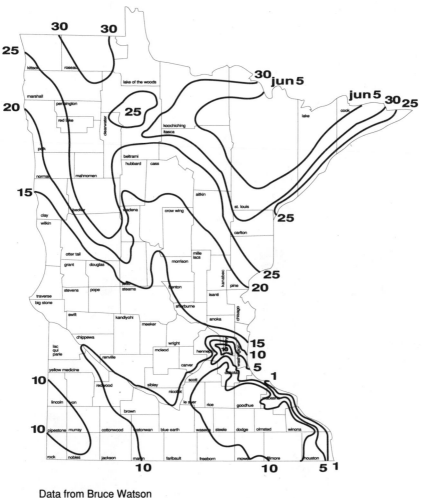

Data from Bruce Watson
© A&WGP

of snow a year, with similar amounts coating western Minnesota up to the Canadian border. Snowfalls are generally in the 4' to 5' range over Minnesota's northeastern quarter, with more than 5' annually in much of the Arrowhead region.

The heart of Minnesota's snowbelt lies along the North Shore Ridge (or Misquah Hills), which rises 500' to 1,200' above Lake Superior between Duluth and Grand Portage. Along the ridge's crest, snowfalls approach 6' per year, with some favored spots, like Isabella, receiving upwards of 100". The heaviest average annual snowfall reported in Minnesota was 107", measured between 1931 and 1950 at the little town of Pigeon River, a few miles inland from Grand Portage. Unfortunately, there are not enough reporting stations in these hills to reveal Minnesota's true snowfall capital.

If ice were not lighter than water, Minnesota would enjoy no scenes such as the concentration of this mid-1950s ice fisherman.

FIRST FROST
(all dates Sept. unless otherwise noted)

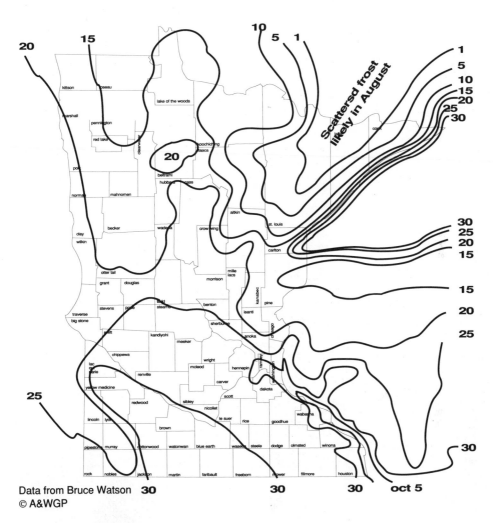

Data from Bruce Watson
© A&WGP

This snowbelt owes its existence to Lake Superior and to the hills themselves. Most snowstorms in Minnesota fall during periods when northeast, east, or southeast winds blow around a passing cyclone. Winds blowing from these directions pick up an extra shot of moisture as they cross the open waters of Lake Superior, and get an upward shove as they blow ashore and up and over the hills. The added moisture and extra uplift provide a double whammy that results in the narrow snowbelt.

Sleet is not all that common in Minnesota, occurring about four or five times a year for most locations. Glaze, or freezing rain, is more common. Western Minnesota gets glazed about 10 times a year, on the average, while the northeastern part of the state may see ice storms 13 or 14 times annually. Fortunately, most of these are light coatings of ice.

Hail, while relatively rare everywhere, is memorable. Most places in Minnesota get hailed upon two or three times a year, on the average. The northeastern tip of the Arrowhead sees hail barely once a year, though. On the other extreme, Minnesota's "hail alley" is in the extreme southwestern corner, where stones fall three to four times a year. The weather station at Sibley, Iowa, a few miles south of Nobles County, recorded 94 hailstorms in 20 years. That's 4.7 storms per year, on the average, making it likely that towns like Worthington and Luverne receive more hail than any other locale in Minnesota.

SUMMER STORMS

■■■■■■■■■■■■■■■■■■■■■■■■■■■■■

Minnesotans seem to enjoy winter, but by March most (even if they won't admit it) have grown a little tired (or plenty sick) of it, and start looking forward to spring. Spring approaches with melting snow and ice breaking up in lakes, and arrives with robins and tiny green leaves bursting from tree buds. But to those who look to the skies to follow the seasons, one of the sweetest sounds in all of nature is that first distant rumble of thunder on a balmy April afternoon. The first thunderstorm of the year doesn't have to come in April, mind you. It's just as likely to show up in late March, and some years there's the odd wintertime thunderstorm (or thunder-snow storm).

Sometimes you have to wait until May for that first boom of spring, although by then the thunderstorm season is usually in high gear. Once or twice a week, on the average, from May through September, Minnesotans are treated to the wonder and spectacle of thunder, lightning and general commotion of these storms. It's less of a treat, of course, if your house is struck by lightning or damaging winds, but for the most part thunderstorms bring welcome rains when they're needed the most—during the crop growing season.

On the average, the annual number of thunderstorms in Minnesota ranges from about 55 in the south to 35 or 40 in the extreme northwest. A more commonly recorded statistic is the number of days with thunderstorms, or "thunderstorm days," which averages 40 to 45 in the south and about 35 in the northwest (some days have two or more storms). For comparison, there are 100 thunderstorm days in central Florida and up to 80 in parts of the Rocky Mountains in Colorado and New Mexico. On the other extreme, Sacramento, California, averages but one thunderstorm day per year, and along the Arctic coast of Alaska, Point Barrow gets about one thunderstorm per decade.

Anything that happens 35 to 55 times per year may seem commonplace. However, consider this: the average thunderstorm runs about an hour, so the 50 storms that rattle the Twin Cities each year last a total of 50 hours (approximately). So, out of the 8,760 hours in a year, only 50—or 0.6 percent—are occupied by thunderstorms. That means that 99.4 percent of the time there isn't a thunderstorm! Meteorologically speaking, thunderstorms are actually quite rare, and require a very special circumstance: "instability."

■■■■■■■■■■■■■■■■

BIRTH OF A THUNDERSTORM

Instability means the atmosphere is unstable. Examples of unstable situations abound in the world around us—a rock perched on a ledge, a cocked gun, an egg balanced on its end, a loaded mouse trap—all ready to go off at the slightest provocation. In each case, the effect exceeds the immediate cause, and once the reaction is triggered and the energy is spent, the situation (usually) becomes stable (at least for a while). Since the world also abounds with little provocations, most unstable situations don't last very long, and most of the time, most things are stable.

Normally, the atmosphere is stable. Cold air in a valley—an inversion—is stable, since the cold air is on the bottom. Cold air is "heavier," or more accurately, denser (meaning more air molecules per cubic foot), than warm air. In essence, the "lighter" warm air floats on top of the cold air—it's the same thing that keeps hot air balloons up. If you try to lift some cold air, say, 100 feet off the ground, you'll find that it will be surrounded by warmer, lighter air. Let it go, and the cold air sinks back to the valley floor. Rising currents don't go very far in stable air.

With unstable air, the temperature drops off fairly rapidly with height—about 25° Fahrenheit per mile. If a blob of air is lifted off the ground, it expands and cools as the pressure around it decreases. However, despite the cooling, the lifted blob remains warmer than the air around it, and keeps going up. Instability is even stronger if there's water vapor in the air to release its latent heat. If you give an upward kick to air in an unstable air layer, it continues to soar upward in a relatively warm stream.

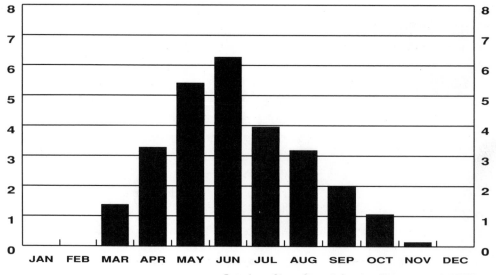

MINNESOTA HAIL STORMS
10-year number for an average location

Data from Glenn Stout & Stanley Changnon © A&WGP

HAIL DAYS PER YEAR

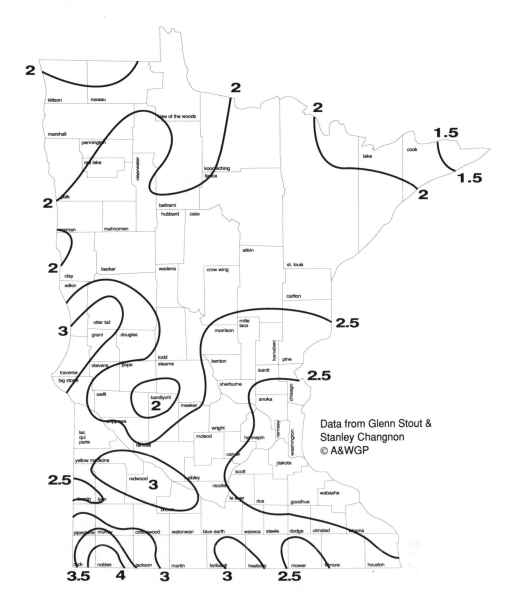

Data from Glenn Stout &
Stanley Changnon
© A&WGP

If the air is moist enough, the rising air stream may become a thunderstorm. As it rises, expands and cools, water vapor (which is a gas) in the air condenses into tiny droplets of liquid water, and a cloud is born.

The condensation of gaseous water vapor into liquid water actually heats up the air in our blob. This is the opposite of evaporation, when liquid water cools its surroundings as it evaporates into vapor (if you've ever stepped out of a swimming pool on a breezy day, you know what I mean). Warming the blob makes it rise a little bit faster. By now, I'll bet you

MEAN ANNUAL PRECIPITATION, INCHES
1951-1970

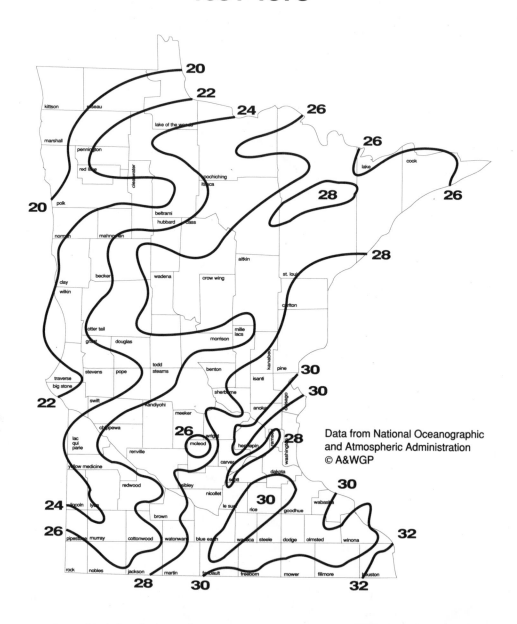

Data from National Oceanographic
and Atmospheric Administration
© A&WGP

can see where this is headed—as the blob rises faster, more condensation occurs, causing it to rise faster yet, and so on. We see these rising blobs as growing cauliflower clouds. Back near the ground, more moist air is drawn into the base of the cloud to keep the condensation going. This process of rising, condensation, heating and faster-rising currents is called "convection." Like combustion in the cylinders of a car engine, it's what keeps thunderstorms going.

Many situations provoke an unstable atmosphere into making a thunderstorm, all of which involve some initial upward shove that starts the cycle of condensation, rising currents, and convection. For many thunderstorms, the updrafts begin with air heated by the sunlit ground below (these are your typical scattered afternoon thundershowers). Some storms, though, get their kick from the up-and-down air currents in different sections of cyclones, especially where the cold front wedges under the moist air and shoves it upward or along the warm front, where the humid air rides up and over the cold air. These "frontal" thunderstorms (ones that form along warm or cold fronts) are often the most severe, sometimes bringing hail, high winds, and tornadoes. Also, virtually all winter thunderstorms are "frontal."

Fronts and sunlight are the intuitively most obvious ways to start a thunderstorm, but many have more unusual causes. For example, many thunderstorms don't get going until the sun goes down. This is especially true in western and southern Minnesota, where more thunderstorms occur at night than during the day (the hourly peak is between 10 p.m. and midnight). The cause here is the exact opposite of that of the solar-powered daytime thunderstorms: clouds and haze layers several miles up radiate their heat out to space, cooling the atmosphere at cloud-top level. Cooling aloft at night has the same effect as heating the ground by day, namely, the atmosphere becomes unstable and air starts rising. Many times both processes go on, with the sun "priming" the atmosphere during the afternoon and the nighttime cloud-top cooling finally setting the storms off a few hours after sundown. The results can be some real doozies. Those caught beneath one of these storms get lots of rain

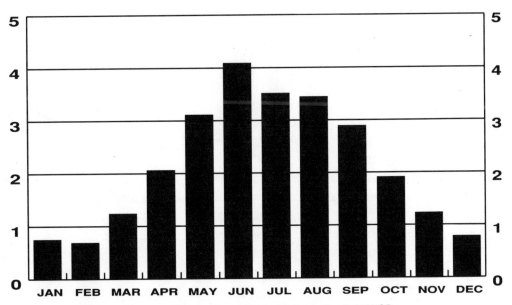

MINNESOTA AVERAGE MONTHLY PRECIPITATION
Statewide averages, 1885-1990

Data from National Oceanographic and Atmospheric Administration © A&WGP

and little sleep, while miles away spectators sit on their porches and watch "heat lightning" light up the sky.

Like the rest of us mortals, thunderstorms have life cycles of birth, growth, the primes of their lives, and death. Many of the meanest storms start out as cotton-like "cumulus" clouds that look like little lambs loitering in the sky. If the air is moist and unstable enough, and the right trigger comes along, one of these puffy cumulus clouds starts growing into a billowing cauliflower, or "towering cumulus."

The atmosphere gets colder as you go higher, and three or four miles up (lower in the winter) the temperature drops below freezing. Now ice crystals, rather than liquid water droplets, result from condensation. The top of the cauliflower cloud assumes a fuzzy and fibrous appearance that is characteristic of ice clouds. High winds aloft may whip ice crystals from the main cloud into a flat, spreading cap often called an "anvil" cloud.

With the appearance of ice crystals, the growing cloud becomes an entirely new animal. Ice crystals are much more efficient than water droplets at grabbing moisture from the air, and are even quite capable of stealing moisture from the droplets themselves. The ice crystals grow rapidly, eventually becoming snowflakes, which fall and melt into rain. Virtually all of Minnesota's rain—even that which turns to steam when it lands on a sun-baked highway—starts out as snow! Now that it's raining, we can add the Latin word "nimbus" (meaning rain) to our cumulus cloud, and call the cloud a "cumulonimbus." *Zap!*

LIGHTNING IN ALL ITS GLORY

The cumulonimbus cloud is not just a cloud; it's a storm. And not just a storm, but a thunderstorm! Thunder (and lightning) result from the same ice crystals that make most of the rain. For a poorly understood reason, when liquid water droplets freeze into ice, electrical charges develop. Ice crystals become positively charged, while the remaining liquid droplets take on a negative charge. Soon the whole cloud becomes charged. Positive charges collect in the icy cloud top and negative charges accumulate in the lower, warmer parts of the cloud. Normally the ground is also negatively charged, but the concentration of electrons in the lower cloud repels the negative ground charge (like charges repel; opposites attract), leaving a positively charged ground directly beneath the cloud. The gathering electrical charges build voltages as high as 100 million volts within the cloud and between cloud and ground. Air is pretty good at holding electrical charges apart. In clouds, air can separate voltages at the rate of 3,000 volts per foot, or 15 million volts per mile. However, when 100 million volts show up, sparks fly.

First a relatively weak and invisible "leader stroke" makes its way down from the base of the cloud. One hundredth of a second later the leader stroke reaches a tree, antenna, the ground, or sometimes several targets, and an electrical pathway—a wire of sorts—connects the cloud and ground. A massive "return stroke" shoots up along the leader path at one sixth the speed of light. Return strokes may rise from each of several ground targets to join several hundred feet up, forming branched lightning. The concentration of electricity in a path a few inches across heats the air almost instantaneously to tens of thousands of degrees—

NORMAL PRECIPITATION
MAY THROUGH SEPTEMBER
(Growing season)

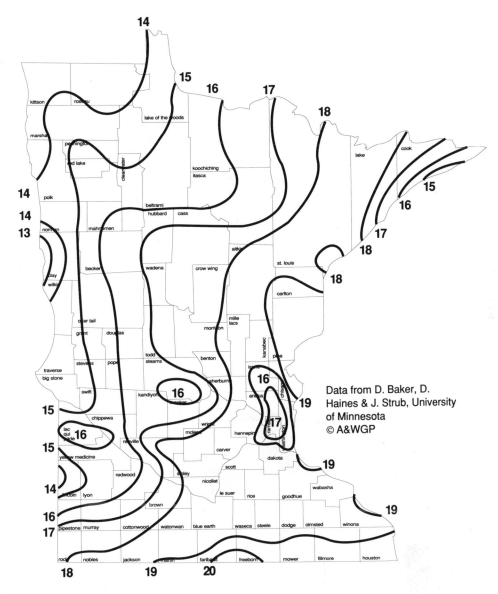

Data from D. Baker, D. Haines & J. Strub, University of Minnesota © A&WGP

several times hotter (and brighter) than the surface of the sun! We see the glowing channel as lightning, while the sudden heating and expansion of the air—essentially a mile-long explosion—makes thunder.

The sight and sound of lightning and thunder are produced simultaneously, but light zips along at 186,000 miles per second, much faster than sound's slow 1,000 *feet* per second (or one mile in 5 seconds). We see lightning a fraction of a blink after it happens, but the rumble of thunder may take several (or many) seconds to reach our ears. This allows you to do some low-tech meteorology. Count the number of seconds between the flash and the boom, divide by five, and you've got your distance from the storm in miles. Do this every few minutes and you can deduce whether the storm is moving toward or away from you, and even predict when it will arrive.

We're most familiar with "cloud-to-ground" lightning which, of course, zaps from the cloud to the ground. However, 90 percent of all lightning stays inside the cloud, and is known as (naturally) "inside cloud" lightning. There's also "cloud-to-cloud" lightning that connects oppositely charged parts of two different clouds. Those diffuse flashes in the sky popularly known as heat (or sheet) lightning are simply the reflection by clouds and air of ordinary lightning too distant to be seen directly. Finally, there's the newly-discovered (thanks to lightning detector networks) "positive" lightning that goes from positively-charged icy cloud tops to the negatively-charged ground several miles away from the storm. Positive lightning is particularly deceptive because is can appear to come out of a clear sky, literally a "bolt from the blue." Also, since they come from the cloud top, not the base, they have to travel farther and are proportionally more energetic. This "new" kind of lightning is something to think about when the sun comes out and a rainbow appears, but the storm is still only a few miles away.

All lightning uses a lot of energy and uses it very quickly. For a few millionths of a second the instantaneous peak rate of energy usage may exceed a trillion watts, equivalent to the average consumption rate of the entire United States. But lightning strokes are incredibly brief, and the total electrical energy expended by an average lightning flash is several hundred kilowatt hours. If you were to buy lightning from Northern States Power, it would cost about $50 per flash. Networks of lightning detectors have found that an average square mile of Minnesota is struck by lightning 10 to 15 times a year. That means Minnesota's 79,285 square miles receive a million strikes a year, or about $50 million worth of electricity.

A total of 137 Minnesotans were struck by lightning between 1959 and 1989. This statistic includes 51 deaths and 86 reported injuries, but there are undoubtedly many unreported minor injuries and quite a few good scares. Factor in the population of Minnesota (4 million) and our average life span (75 years or so), and the average Minnesotan's odds of being struck by lightning sometime in his or her life are one in 12,000. (Now you can put a number behind the proverbial "about as likely as getting hit by lightning.") Many of those killed and injured by lightning were engaged in outdoor activities such as boating (9 reported in 31 years), golfing (9), and working near tractors or road equipment (7). Twenty-eight Minnesotans were struck while standing beneath trees, but the greatest number (30) were hit by lightning in open fields or baseball parks. However, even some indoor activities can be dangerous during a thunderstorm—13 Minnesotans talking on the telephone have been struck by lightning coming "over the wires." These statistics give a pretty clear idea of what people should *not* do during thunderstorms.

■ ■ ■ ■ ■ ■ ■ ■ ■ ■ ■ ■ ■ ■ ■ ■

STORMY WEATHER

Continuing with the saga of our storm, the thunderstorm is now crackling with lightning and dropping some rain. It is now also capable of producing some of Minnesota's most destructive weather. While the cumulus was growing, its air currents were all heading upward. But as rain began to fall, so did some of the air. When the rain-laden downdrafts reach the ground, they spread out, and we enjoy the first gusts of cool air that break the heat on an August afternoon. Sometimes, though, these gusts can get out of hand and exceed 100 m.p.h., wrecking roofs and toppling trees. On other occasions the downdrafts may be concentrated in a column less than a mile (sometimes only a few hundred yards) across. The powerful downdraft hits the ground like a garden hose spraying a wall, spreading out in all directions at speeds of 50 or 100 m.p.h. or even higher. People and things on the ground experience sudden, localized, short-lived, and rapidly changing winds—brief tempests known as a "microbursts." On the ground microbursts can cause severe local damage that mimics that of a tornado, but the greatest threat is to aircraft flying through the shifting winds. Several recent airline disasters (none in Minnesota) have been attributed to microbursts. Experimental weather detection systems, including wind gauge networks and Doppler radar (which can pick up motions in the atmosphere) are due to be installed at many airports during the 1990s, making the skies a safer place.

Eventually, the supply of moist air that feeds the storm runs out, having fallen as rain or hail, and the thunderstorms begins to fade. Updrafts within the cloud weaken and finally cease, leaving only sinking currents of rain- and snow-filled air. The cloud's edges turn ragged as they begin to evaporate. Above, the icy anvil cloud may separate and blow off with the high-level winds, while below, light rain falls out of a disappearing cloud. The typical life cycle of growth, storm, and decay runs one to three hours.

Not all storms fade so fast. Thunderstorms pushed along by cold fronts are continually shoved into the moist air mass, while some slow-moving storms may tap a steady flow of moisture blowing in from afar. In either case the action can go on for many hours or the better part of a day. Some of the longest-lived thunderstorms line up like halfbacks and march forward into the moist air, scooping up fresh water vapor as they go. The approach of one of these "squall lines" can be an imposing spectacle, with a wall of dark, thundering clouds stretching from horizon to horizon. Squall lines often develop along cold fronts, but often outrun the front and take off on their own. Other thunderstorms may congregate in enormous "Mesoscale Convective Complexes," or MCC's (maybe someday we'll have a snazzier name). MCC's may grow 100 or 200 miles across and live 12 to 24 hours, with new thunderstorms continually popping up to replace old, dying storms. The total rainfall from one of these systems can exceed that of a hurricane, and MCC's have unleashed more than one flash flood on Minnesota's waterways.

TORNADO!

■■■■■■■■■■■■■■■■■■■■■■■■■■■■■■■■

The afternoon of Friday, July 18, 1986 was about as warm and sticky as Minnesota afternoons get. To Scott Woelm, an amateur radio operator and volunteer weather watcher for the Twin Cities area "Skywarn" group, muggy days mean the possibility of severe weather, but the heat got the better of him and he dozed off in front of the television. He didn't doze long—the silence was broken at 4:50 p.m. by a beeping bulletin, announcing a tornado touchdown in Brooklyn Park, about five miles from his home in Blaine, north of Minneapolis. Several minutes later another bulletin placed the tornado near a shopping mall one mile away! Severe weather can break out anywhere in Minnesota, and on most "storm chases" Woelm drives quite a few miles to see—and report—what's going on. This time the chase was a 30-second walk to the nearest street corner. As Woelm said,

"I could not believe my eyes. There it was! Right square in front of me. About a mile out and just hanging there, a nozzle-shaped tornado was doing its dance for all to see. For the next 20 minutes a small group of us watched as it built up in strength. Above us scud clouds spun around like the 'wave' at a hockey game. We were all fascinated by the eerie silence and only on a few occasions did we actually hear the roar of the tornado.

"Soon after the tornado reached its peak it began to dissipate into the 'rope' stage. As it weakened it went 'sideways' to a position right above us! It spun around for about two minutes. I stood there, too frozen to capture it on film, and watched it until it disappeared."

What Woelm saw was possibly the most photographed tornado of all time. As he observed from the streets, hundreds of thousands of others watched the spectacle broadcast live on television from a KARE-TV traffic helicopter. Although it touched down in the Minneapolis–St. Paul metropolitan area, damage was relatively light and there were no injuries. The twister spent most of its life tearing up trees at the Springbrook Nature Center, half a mile from developed land.

Minnesotans aren't always so lucky when it comes to tornadoes. Since the territory's first recorded tornado in 1820, at least 400 Minnesotans—and probably many more—have lost their lives to these violent whirlwinds.

In 1931 a tornado targeted the Great Northern railroad's "Empire Builder" train near Moorhead, tossing an 83-ton coach car, with 117 passengers aboard, 80 feet from the tracks.

NUMBER OF TORNADOES PER CENTURY
Passing within 5 miles

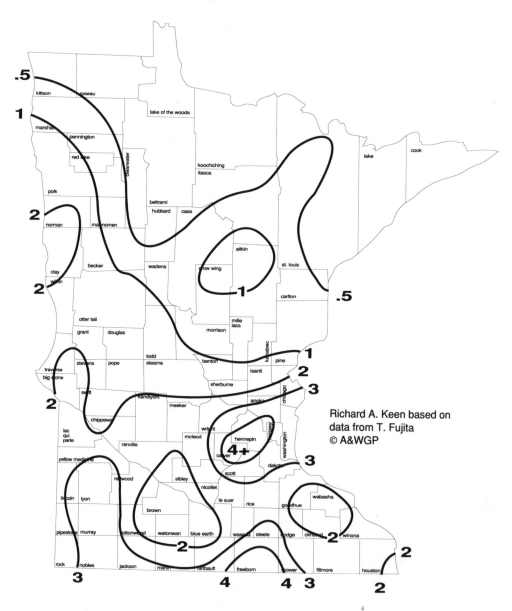

Richard A. Keen based on
data from T. Fujita
© A&WGP

The massive tornado that flattened half of Fergus Falls on June 22, 1919, split open a tree, threw an automobile into the opening, and then pushed the tree parts back together, crushing the car. The same storm also plucked a clothes trunk from one house and placed it, undamaged, in the attic of another house two blocks away. Yet, tornadoes can be strangely merciful: in 1954 a tornado-borne farmer in Harding flew 40 feet into the air and landed unhurt.

Tornadoes are the most powerful storms on earth, and they are frightening, fascinating, deadly, beautiful and quirky. Fortunately, they are also rare. Tornadoes require very special meteorological conditions to develop. Among these are moist low-level air overrun by drier air aloft, strong instability, a strong jet stream aloft, a change in wind direction and speed between the lower and upper levels of the troposphere, and some pre-existing rotation in the lowest layers of air. All of these conditions may be found in the warm sectors of strong cyclones, while a sufficient number of these conditions to generate tornadoes might be found elsewhere.

Like nowhere else on earth, these special conditions are found in the central part of the United States in an area known as "Tornado Alley." More than half of the world's annual average of 1,000 tornadoes touch down in the central United States, making the tornado more American than baseball and hot dogs!

Over the past century tornadoes have killed between 15,000 and 20,000 Americans, but deaths have decreased in recent years, thanks to improved forecasting and warning systems. During the decade of the 1980s the human loss from tornadoes in the U.S. averaged about 60 per year. Meanwhile, property damage due to tornadoes has steadily increased to an annual loss of $1 billion or more in most years since 1973.

Minnesota lies at the very northern end of Tornado Alley. With an average of 18 tornadoes per year since 1953, Minnesota ranks 18th among the states. Even so, those 18 tornadoes put Minnesota well ahead of Australia's 14 and Japan's 11 tornadoes, and only slightly behind the 25 or so per year reported from Italy, New Zealand and Great Britain. The frequency of tornadoes drops off rapidly as one heads north across the state. A farm-

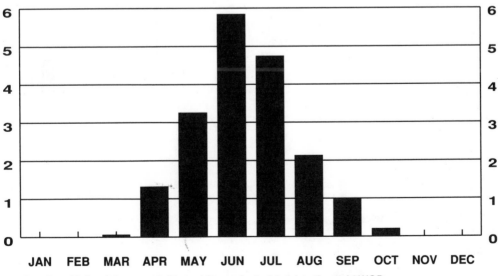

MINNESOTA TORNADOES
Average for each month, 1959-1989

Data from National Oceanographic and Atmospheric Administration © A&WGP

house in southern Minnesota is five times more likely to be damaged by a tornado than is a cabin in the north woods. More tornadoes have touched down in Los Angeles than in any similarly-sized chunk of northeastern Minnesota, and at the point of the Arrowhead, Cook County has never seen a tornado.

To everything there is a season, and for tornadoes the season to be wary is late spring and early summer. This is when the conducive conditions of warmth, humidity, winds aloft, and so on are most likely to occur together. Fourteen of the year's 18 tornadoes (on the average) touch down in May, June and July, with the peak month—June—hosting six of them. Tornadoes are late risers, too, and very few are seen before noon. Only 8 percent of all Minnesota tornadoes occur between midnight and noon, while the peak hours of 4 p.m. to 7 p.m. (Central Standard Time) catch 43 percent of the total. The reason is, of course, that the sun heats the lower atmosphere during the day, making it hotter, lighter, more unstable, and ready to rise.

So now it's 5 p.m. on a June afternoon, and Minnesota lies in the warm sector of a late spring cyclone approaching from the west. All the conditions are ripe for tornado develop-ment, and the National Weather Service has issued a Tornado Watch. Somewhere in Minnesota, a thunderstorm is born. Its powerful updrafts (due to moisture and instability) draw in the slowly rotating air circulating around the cyclone. This concentrates the spin-ning motion, like water swirling faster as it approaches a drain. As the updraft strengthens, the spinning speeds up, until the updraft becomes a narrow, rotating column—a tornado.

In exceptional cases, the whole thunderstorm may start rotating, becoming a parent cloud capable of spawning tornadoes every few minutes for an hour or more. These awe-some "supercell" (or "mesocyclone") thunderstorms ravage the Midwest many times every

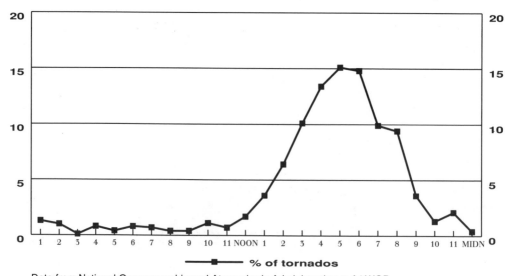

MINNESOTA TORNADOES
Percent occurring each hour of the day

% of tornados

Data from National Oceanographic and Atmospheric Administration © A&WGP

MINNESOTA TORNADO HISTORY

Year	Date	Location	Deaths	Damage $Millions
1879	7/2	Minn./Wis., crossed Mississippi River	14	*
1881	7/15	New Ulm	6	0.4
1883	8/21	Rochester	31	0.2
1884	9/9	White Bear Lake	6	2.0
1886	4/14	St. Cloud/Sauk Rapids	74	0.5
1890	7/13	near St. Paul	6	*
1894	6/27	16 places in Minnesota	10	*
1904	8/20	Downtown Minneapolis & St Paul	14	1.5
1914	8/16	Grant & Stevens counties	2	*
		Swath 1.5 mi wide cleared		
1918	8/21	Tyler	36	1.0
1919	6/22	Fergus Falls	59	3.5
1928	8/20	Freeborn, Mower counties	6	1.0
1929	4/5	Minneapolis	6	1.0
1931	5/27	near Moorhead	1	0.2
		Empire Builder train wrecked		
1939	6/18	Hennepin, Anoka counties	9	1.2
1941	9/4	Minneapolis	6	0.5
1946	8/17	Mankato, Blue Earth County	11	0.2
1951	7/20	Minneapolis–St. Paul	5	6.0
1957	6/20	Fargo-Moorhead	10	13.0
		(most in North Dakota)		
1965	5/6	Sibley to Anoka counties	16	57.0
		6 tornadoes in Twin Cities metro area		
1967	4/30	Albert Lea	12	9.0
		21 tornadoes in Iowa/Minnesota		
1968	6/13	Tracy, SW MN	9	4.0
1969	8/6	North Central	15	4.8
		12 tornadoes		
1978	7/5	Gary, Fosston	4	5.0-50.0
1980	9/3	St. Cloud	1	9.0
1981	6/14	Minneapolis	1	5.0-50.0
1984	4/26	St. Anthony-Mounds View	1	5.0-50.0
1986	7/18	Brooklyn Park		0.7
		Seen live on TV!		

* Damage estimate not available

year, and are responsible for the most lethal tornadoes. Once or twice a decade, a spring-time cyclone heading east from the Rockies spawns supercells and tornadoes by the dozen on its march to the sea. The ensuing atmospheric reign of terror may spread devastation across an area of several states and leave hundreds dead and thousands injured. Several of the massive tornado outbreaks have affected Minnesota.

Tornadoes come in many sizes, shapes and strengths. The largest can be a mile or more across with 300-mile-per-hour winds, and may scour the land along a 50- to 250-mile path before dissipating. Fortunately, these mile-wide monsters are rare, but when they strike, it's a mess. In 1914 a huge tornado cleared out a 1.5-mile-path across Grant and Stevens counties. At the other extreme, tiny twisters may touch down for a few seconds, damaging a single tree or part of a roof before disappearing. I saw one leave a neat but narrow 30-foot wide path in a cornfield, and another with winds barely strong enough to pick up cardboard boxes (although it sent newspapers spiralling thousands of feet up into the base of the thunderstorm!).

The typical tornado, based on nationwide statistics, has winds of 150 m.p.h. swirling around a 700-foot-wide funnel, and moves at 40 m.p.h. over a five-mile-long path during its five- or 10-minute lifetime. Like the 1.9-child family, though, this "typical" tornado is actually the rarest of them all. The appearance of a tornado can vary as much as its size, ranging from fat cylinders to thin, coiling ropes.

The famous funnel cloud results from the condensation of water vapor inside the rotating column, where the pressure and temperature are lower. If the funnel cloud doesn't reach

MINNESOTA ANNUAL TORNADOES
Yearly total 1916-1990

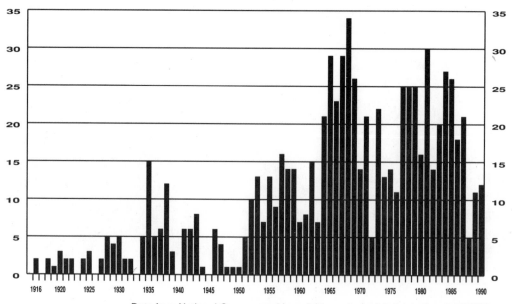

Data from National Oceanographic and Atmospheric Administration © A&WGP

Near Bellingham on July 5, 1939, a tornado touches down and draws up its funnel a dense cloud of dust and debris from the fields.

Fifty-nine residents of Fergus Falls died, and half the town was destroyed, in the 1919 tornado.

all the way to the ground, the rotating tube of air may not go all the way down either or, if it does, its winds at ground level are very weak. In the most powerful storms the base of the thundercloud itself might appear to simply dip to the ground, and at close range the violently churning cloud may bear little resemblance to what most people expect a torna-do to look like. Their disguised appearance, along with their sheer strength, makes these tornadoes the most dangerous of all. Sometimes miniature, snake-like whirlwinds, a few feet across and lasting only seconds, writhe along the fringes of the main funnel. If the funnel is surrounded by rain it might not be visible at all. The classic "Wizard of Oz" elephant trunk funnels are photogenic and popular in weather books, but they're not all that common.

Just as large cyclones spawn rotating supercell thunderstorms, which in turn spin off tornadoes, tornadoes themselves can create even smaller whirls. This tendency for big whirls to make little whirls is one of the great truths of meteorology (ultimately, all this spinning comes from the largest whirl of them all, the earth's rotation!). The small but intense whirlwinds that travel in circular paths around the main whirl of the tornado have been named "suction spots" (because of their action on objects on the ground). Suction spots are typically less than 30 feet across and last only seconds, but account for some of the remark-ably erratic patterns of destruction observed in "multiple-vortex tornadoes." In real life and in videos suction spots can be seen writhing snake-like within the main tornado circulation; in still pictures they appear as streamers and funnel-shaped concentrations at the base of the main funnel.

The smaller and briefer a weather phenomenon is, the harder it is to predict. Because of tornadoes' lethal nature, this difficulty can result in tragedy. Any attempts to forecast these deadly storms therefore are worth the effort. "Tornado prediction is no longer a mere possibility, but in many respects may be considered an accomplished fact. By this I do not mean absolute perfection, but reasonable success." John Finley, of the U.S. Army Signal Corps, wrote these words in 1887. Despite vast advances in our understanding of tornadoes and their causes, they could have been written yesterday.

Over the century since Finley issued his first warnings, forecasters have improved their skills at recognizing the exact conditions—moisture, instability and so on—in which tornadoes are likely to break out. When these conditions occur, the National Weather Service issues a "Tornado Watch" stating that tornadoes are possible in an area 100 or so miles across sometime during the next few hours. Until recently, however, they couldn't issue a Tornado Warning, meaning a twister *will* strike a certain place at a certain time, until someone had actually seen the funnel cloud or the tornado was already on the ground. In the 1990s, the latest in meteorological technology, Doppler Radar, will become operational across the United States. By virtue of its ability to sense wind motions in the atmosphere, and in particular little swirls that may become tornadoes, Doppler Radar may provide up to 20 minutes advance notice of developing twisters. Twenty minutes is not a whole lot of time, considering it takes five or 10 minutes to get the warning out to the public. However, the remaining 10 minutes is still sufficient to get a school full of kids into the basement or hallway.

Above: A sheet of ice, frozen to both the shore and the lake bottom, extends several yards out into Lake Superior near Tofte. Farther out, waves have broken the ice into irregular chunks.

Top: Brisk winds send streamers of snow drifting across a country road in Dahlgren Township. Slightly stronger winds would lift the snow to eye level, creating a "ground blizzard" with reduced visibility, and making driving hazardous.

Above: Branches bow and break under the weight of an accumulation of glaze ice—rain that fell in subfreezing temperatures and froze to whatever it touched.

Left: Two feet of snow buried downtown Excelsior during the Halloween night "Mega-Storm" of 1991.

Above: *Floes of pancake ice fill Agate Bay at Two Harbors. The continuous motion of waves beneath the ice prevents the pancakes from freezing together into a solid pack.*

Right: *Ice is strongest when it's free of air bubbles, but even this crystalline sheet of shore ice buckled under the force of shifting pack ice along Lake Superior.*

Left: *Patterns of built-up internal pressure, due to the expansion of freezing water inside the ice, appear as multi-colored bands in this photograph taken through a polarizing filter.*

Gusty winds blow and light rain falls in streaks from the base of a thunderstorm near Watertown.

Left: *Like wind-generated waves on a lake, shifting winds aloft create ripples in the amosphere. Here, a moist air layer renders the ripples visible as a rows of narrow, billowy clouds.*

Right: *Curtains of "virga," rain that evaporates before reaching the ground, descend from a cloud base over central Minnesota.*

Below: *Thickening layers of translucent altostratus clouds (with the sun dimly visible) and ragged, lower stratocumulus clouds herald an approaching storm over Lake Superior.*

Above: *Thick sheaths of ice crystals top a cumulonimbus cloud with a spreading "anvil" cloud, the mark of a fully grown thunderstorm.*

Top: *A threatening and turbulent cloud base chases boaters and swimmers out of Detroit Lake on July 13, 1972. The brunt of the storm missed this area, but high winds and a tornado damaged nearby Fergus Falls and Wadena.*

The well defined leading edge of this squall over Lake Superior locates the leading edge of a "gust front," the rush of high winds that often immediately precedes a thunderstorm.

JERRY BIELICKI

Cloud-to-ground lightning rakes the skyline of Excelsior. This time exposure caught several strikes.

Electric currents running along the ground from a lightning strike cut these narrow furrows on a golf course in St. Paul. These "ground currents" are the reason lightning doesn't have to hit

Above: High winds on the heels of a wet snowfall rolled the sticky layer up like sleeping bags into "snow rollers." This rare scene is from a lake in Eden Prairie on December 26, 1970.

Left: Flood waters from the Crow River spill into Lippert Lake, submerging this road near appropriately-named Watertown.

ROGER JENSEN

MIKE MAGNUSON

Above: *The tornado that roared through Maple Grove in the late afternoon of July 23, 1987, destroying 14 homes and damaging nearly 300 more, was the beginning of the overnight "Super-storm" that doused the Twin Cities with 10" of rain.*

Top: *A mile-wide tornado rips through the countryside near Moorhead, June 28, 1975. Although several farm buildings were damaged, there were no injuries. However, the rainstorm that followed flooded 4,000 square miles along the Red River.*

Above: *Dry topsoil, desiccated by the great drought of 1988, fills the sky as high wind whips fields near Sleepy Eye, west of New Ulm.*

Top: *Powerful gusts from a rapidly moving thunderstorm snapped some trees off at their bases while uprooting others. Such straight-line winds can pack the wallop of a tornado while lacking the rotational motion.*

A heavy coating of frozen spray encases an ore freighter entering Duluth after crossing Lake Superior in subzero weather.

Above: Streamers of steam, known as "Arctic Sea Smoke," rise from the relatively warm waters of Lake Superior on a subzero day. Sometimes the streamers spin up into tiny, tornado-like "steam devils" that usually are harmless.

Top: "Slush hour" traffic makes its way home over snowy roads in low visibility as a snowstorm engulfs the metropolitan Twin Cities area.

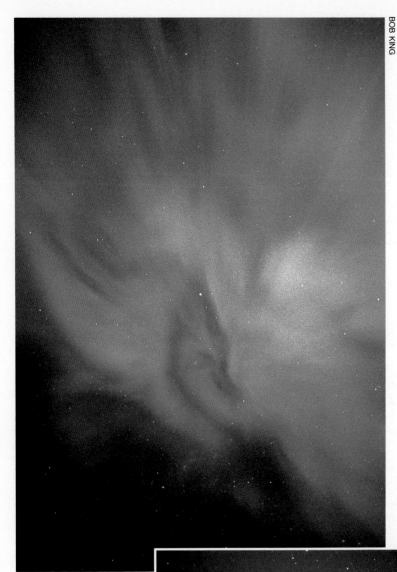

Curtains and rays in the aurora borealis sometimes converge overhead to form a "corona," a phenomenon seen only in the largest displays of the northern lights.

Delicate arcs, some with faint vertical rays, dance across the sky near Shoreview. The arcs may be less than a mile wide, but appear slightly blurred due to their motion during this time exposure.

THE HURRICANE THAT HIT ST. PAUL

Every year, on the average, one or two hurricanes strike the U.S. mainland. This simple statistic keeps millions of coastal residents and vacationers, from Texas to Florida and on up to Maine, on their toes during the "Hurricane Season" of August, September and October. Before the season is over, the odds are that thousands of these people will have their lives shattered by an oceanic onslaught whipped up by what has been called "The Greatest Storm on Earth."

Hurricanes are creatures of the sea, and need the ready supply of moisture that oceans provide to keep themselves going. Most hurricanes break up within hours of landfall. At the closest, Minnesota lies 890 miles from the Atlantic Ocean and 930 miles from the Gulf of Mexico. Of the 50 states, only North Dakota lies farther from salt water. So, we shouldn't expect Minnesota to see hurricanes very often, if at all. Traditional wisdom, however, claims that given enough time, just about anything can happen. A monkey playing with a typewriter might pound out a book on Minnesota's weather, and a hurricane could strike St. Paul. In the case of the hurricane, the unlikely event occurred at the turn of the 20th century, in September 1900.

The culprit storm was first detected on August 27, 1900, over the tropical Atlantic midway between the Caribbean isle of Guadeloupe and the west coast of Africa. With peak winds less than hurricane force (73 m.p.h.), the disturbance was categorized as a "tropical storm." Over the next 10 days the storm plodded steadily westward, skimming the Virgin Islands, Puerto Rico, the Dominican Republic and Haiti, causing minimal damage. It crossed Cuba on the 3rd and 4th, and on the morning of September 5, as it entered the Gulf of Mexico, the storm became a hurricane. During its three-day trek across the steamy waters of the gulf, the new hurricane's power grew rapidly. As it approached the Texas shoreline on the afternoon of the 8th its winds were in excess of 120 m.p.h. Its target was the prosperous coastal resort and business hub, Galveston. The center of the hurricane passed just south of Galveston on the evening of Saturday, September 8. Dawn found the city in ruins, with 6,000 or more of its 40,000 citizens dead, and most of the rest homeless. It was by far the worst meteorological calamity—or any natural disaster—in U.S. history.

Once over Texas, the storm began losing some of its punch, and its winds dropped below hurricane strength as it approached Dallas and Fort Worth. However, the storm refused to die. The weather map on September 10 showed a remarkable feature—a tropical storm over eastern Kansas! That night, as the tropical storm crossed Kansas City and entered Iowa, it merged with a cold front to produce a hybrid low pressure system. As the center of the hybrid low passed from Des Moines to Dubuque, moist tropical air drawn up and over the cold front produced torrential rains north of the storm's path. At St. Paul three days of heavy rains amounted to a whopping 6.65". Bird Island received 7.91", and on the day with the heaviest rains—September 11—Pleasant Mounds was doused with 5.50". Fortunately for Minnesota, winds were fairly light during the drenching, and relatively little damage was reported.

The storm still wasn't finished, however. It grew in strength as it approached Milwaukee, and nearly sank a steamer with 300 on board as both were crossing Lake Michigan. Chicago was lashed by sustained winds of 72 m.p.h. (nearly hurricane force), and probable higher gusts. Two days later and 1,500 miles farther east, the still raging cyclone wrecked 22 fishing boats and drowned 14 fishermen along the coast of Newfoundland. On September 16 the finally dying storm center was situated over the polar ice north of Iceland.

During its three-week rampage from the tropical Atlantic to the ice-covered Arctic, this incredible tempest unleashed human suffering along its 7,000-mile-long track. Minnesota was certainly spared the worst of the storm, but St. Paul's 6-inch-plus rainfall remains on the record books as the Capital City's soggiest rainstorm ever.

Was this storm a fluke, or can we expect another hurricane to pay a visit to Minnesota some day? Several times this century, soggy tropical air masses remaining from tropical storms have brought thunderstorms to Minnesota, but these were nothing like the great Galveston storm. A near-miss occurred in 1961, when Hurricane Carla stormed ashore 100 miles west of Galveston (with far fewer fatalities) and tracked north across Missouri and Illinois. Iowa and Wisconsin were soaked with 2" to 6" of rain, but the heaviest rains in extreme southeastern Minnesota totaled only about an inch. By following a path 200 miles southeast of the 1900 storm, Carla missed Minnesota. While the 1900 storm brought heavy rains to Minnesota, its high winds remained just south of the state. Should a similar storm follow a path 200 miles farther to the northwest, parts of Minnesota could receive hurricane-force winds. It would be a rare event indeed, but in meteorology, rare never means impossible!

This St. Paul Pioneer-Press *illustration of September 13, 1900 explained how the hurricane known especially for devastating Galveston, Texas could also affect Minnesota. In all, the storm traveled about 7,000 miles overland.*

LOCAL CLIMATE DATA

■■■■■■■■■■■■■■■■■■■■■■■■■■■■■

It's certainly interesting to know where Minnesota's hottest, coldest, rainiest, and snowiest places are. For most people, though, it's even more interesting to know these details about their home towns, or of wherever they're going to visit or vacation. Not every road crossing and hamlet in Minnesota has its own weather station, but here's a list of climate data for most of those places that do.

The data come from a variety of sources, including the National Climate Data Center in Asheville, North Carolina, the University of Minnesota Agricultural Experiment Station, and even some individuals, such as Bruce F. Watson, Tom St. Martin, Steve Reckers, Dave Wierstad, Jonathan Cohen and others who run their own weather stations.

Some of the locations are major (or minor) urban centers, in or near which many readers might live. Wherever the weather observations are taken at the airport, the letters "AP" follow the town name. Some of the major weather stations are operated by the National Weather Service and the Federal Aviation Administration, and many others are located at hospitals, dams, parks, and even sewage plants. A large number of weather stations, however, are run by interested families and individuals. We owe these volunteers an enormous debt of gratitude for their long-term efforts, without which our knowledge of Minnesota's climate would be much less complete. Perhaps this may inspire you to set up your own weather station—after five or 10 years, you can add your own climate data to this table.

Just for grins, I added Moscow (the one in Russia) to the list. Of all the major cities in the world, Moscow's climate most closely resembles that of Minnesota (globe-trotting Minnesotans take note!). For the benefit of sailors and boaters, I've thrown in some very approximate climate statistics for the open waters of Lake Superior (based on shipboard weather observations in the vicinity of a point 40 miles south of Grand Portage). Superior's water temperature typically varies from an even freezing (32°) in February and March to a peak in the 53° to 55° range during August and early September.

Modern weather stations can produce a bewildering variety of data. The more relevant and interesting statistics include:

Elevation (feet)—Along with latitude, elevation is one of the most important factors in determining a place's climate. Except right along the shores of Lake Superior, it generally gets colder as you go higher. The cooling rate averages 1° for every 400 feet in winter, and 1° for every 180 feet in summer (this from a study by Donald Baker and others at the University of Minnesota).

Year Records Begin—The longer weather records have been taken, the more reliable the averages will be. It takes about 10 or 20 years to come up with a truly representative average. For comparing one place with another, it's best to compute averages over the same period of years. Most, but not all, of the averages listed here are for the most recent "official" averaging period, 1951 through 1980. Some weather stations closed down before 1980 or opened up after 1951, in which cases some other averaging period (obviously) had to be chosen.

Average Temperature (Fahrenheit)—Annual average temperatures to be fairly worthless at describing a place's climate—the 44° annual average at Minneapolis-St. Paul is closely matched by Glasgow, Scotland; Flagstaff, Arizona; Ketchikan, Alaska; and Aspen, Colorado. None of these places has summers or winters quite like those found in Minnesota, even though the averages are the same. Listed here are the average daily high and low temperatures for July and January, which give a much better picture of the daily and seasonal ranges of temperature.

Temperature Extremes—These are the highest and lowest temperatures since records began. The longer the period of record, the more extreme the extremes are likely to be. In particular, most of Minnesota's all-time high temperatures were set in July 1936, and any weather station that was not around during that summer is likely to have a lower record high temperature than other nearby locations.

Last/First Freezing Temperature in Spring/Fall—These are average dates of the last and first 32° overnight minimum temperatures, and give an idea of when tender plants can go into the ground and when they need to be harvested or brought inside. In half the years the actual first or last freeze occurs within 10 days of the average date, but in extreme years the freeze can be up to 3 or 4 weeks "off schedule." Being below the ground, many seeds can be planted before the last spring freeze, while root vegetables and other hardy plants may keep growing past the first autumn freeze.

Average Annual Precipitation (inches)—Precipitation includes the water contained in snow, hail, sleet, etc., along with what fell as rain. As a rule, 10" of snow melts down to 1" of precipitation.

Average Annual Snowfall (inches)—This totals the snowfalls of all the individual storms in a year.

MINNESOTA LOCAL CLIMATE DATA

STATION	ELEV.	YEAR RECORDS BEGIN	AVERAGE TEMP. JULY MAX.	AVERAGE TEMP. JULY MIN.	AVERAGE TEMP. JAN. MAX.	AVERAGE TEMP. JAN. MIN.	TEMPERATURE EXTREMES HIGH	TEMPERATURE EXTREMES LOW	LAST/FIRST FREEZING TEMP. SPRING	LAST/FIRST FREEZING TEMP. FALL	AVERAGE ANNUAL PRECIP.	AVERAGE ANNUAL SNOW
Ada	906	1898	82	57	13	-7	111	-53	May 23	Sep 20	22.85	29.7
Albert Lea	1235	1885	82	62	21	3	106	-41	May 3	Oct 6	30.57	37.9
Alexandria AP	1421	1895	81	60	15	-4	105	-47	May 11	Sep 29	24.59	39.2
Argyle	845	1917	81	54	11	-10	107	-43	May 24	Sep 17	19.01	34.1
Artichoke Lake	1075	1917	83	60	17	-3	109	-39	May 12	Sep 26	23.60	35.6
Austin	1215	1939	82	60	20	1	102	-42	May 8	Oct 4	31.12	39.4
Babbitt	1615	1924	76	55	13	-5	103	-41	May 20	Sep 24	28.00	58.8
Baudette	1075	1911	77	54	11	-12	103	-52	May 26	Sep 15	22.59	56.2
Beardsley	1090	1898	85	58	23	0	115	-41	May 7	Sep 23	21.36	36.1
Bemidji AP	1392	1919	79	56	13	-10	107	-50	May 29	Sep 13	22.72	39.3
Big Falls	1220	1934	79	52	14	-11	106	-53	June 4	Sep 6	25.95	58.0
Bird Island	1089	1889	85	61	21	2	106	-38	May 9	Sep 30	28.17	41.8
Brainerd	1214	1908	81	59	20	-2	106	-46	May 6	Sep 24	26.95	58.0
Caledonia	1170	1904	82	61	23	6	104	-35	May 2	Oct 2	34.25	37.9
Cambridge	1000	1934	82	59	18	-2	109	-42	May 12	Sep 27	28.59	42.4
Campbell	975	1905	83	57	16	-4	111	-40	May 18	Sep 22	21.83	39.4
Canby	1243	1918	86	60	21	1	111	-33	May 8	Sep 30	24.86	37.5
Chaska/Shakopee	726	1916	84	61	21	1	109	-43	May 7	Sep 28	28.60	38.8
Cloquet	1265	1911	78	53	16	-5	105	-45	June 6	Sep 4	29.96	68.9
Collegeville	1225	1893	81	60	17	-2	106	-39	May 10	Sep 29	28.37	37.5
Crookston	883	1893	81	57	11	-8	106	-51	May 19	Sep 21	20.03	36.2
Detroit Lakes	1375	1896	79	55	13	-9	107	-53	May 22	Sep 19	23.78	38.9
Duluth AP	1409	1942	76	54	16	-3	97	-39	May 22	Sep 24	29.68	76.8
Duluth City	1128	1875	75	54	18	0	106	-41	May 13	Oct 3	29.63	56.2
Fairmont	1187	1887	84	62	21	3	109	-35	May 5	Oct 8	29.19	41.5
Faribault	1190	1897	83	60	20	1	108	-37	May 6	Oct 5	31.03	43.0
Farmington	902	1888	82	60	19	0	110	-40	May 9	Oct 1	29.74	41.9
Fergus Falls	1210	1892	82	58	14	-5	110	-42	May 13	Sep 25	23.52	41.7
Fosston	1289	1910	80	56	13	-8	110	-48	May 24	Sep 16	22.71	31.7
Grand Forks AP, ND	830	1889	82	56	11	-7	109	-44	May 20	Sep 23	19.57	39.7
Grand Marais	688	1916	70	51	20	1	100	-34	May 23	Sep 29	26.40	56.3
Grand Meadow	1338	1886	81	59	21	3	107	-39	May 10	Sep 29	31.64	44.4
Grand Rapids	1281	1915	78	54	15	-7	104	-51	May 29	Sep 8	26.36	57.0
Gull Lake Dam	1215	1911	80	58	16	-5	107	-47	May 16	Sep 26	26.29	49.4
Hallock	813	1899	81	55	10	-10	109	-51	May 28	Sep 14	19.30	32.3

STATION	ELEV.	YEAR RECORDS BEGIN	AVERAGE TEMP. JULY MAX.	JULY MIN.	JAN. MAX.	JAN. MIN.	TEMPERATURE EXTREMES HIGH	LOW	LAST/FIRST FREEZING TEMP. SPRING	FALL	AVERAGE ANNUAL PRECIP.	SNOW
Hibbing/Mahoning	1578	1921	74	55	19	1	102	-40	May 19	Sep 24	29.77	66.2
Hinckley	1035	1922	80	55	17	-4	104	-41	May 19	Sep 24	29.27	48.0
Internat'l Falls AP	1179	1896	79	54	11	-11	103	-49	May 23	Sep 17	24.35	60.7
Itasca State Park	1500	1912	80	53	15	-10	105	-51	June 4	Sep 8	26.23	46.6
Jordan	930	1949	82	59	19	0	105	-41	May 2	Oct 6	28.13	34.7
La Crosse AP, WI	651	1872	84	62	23	5	108	-43	Apr 25	Oct 16	30.25	41.6
Lake Superior	602	1960	67	49	27	15	88	-8*			29.00	120.0
Leech Lake Dam	1301	1887	79	56	15	-7	104	-59	May 26	Sep 16	24.65	58.1
Litchfield	1132	1939	82	60	18	-1	104	-34	May 10	Sep 28	26.96	43.8
Little Falls	1115	1910	81	58	17	-5	106	-46	May 10	Sep 26	26.38	37.0
Long Prairie	1289	1913	81	57	15	-6	105	-45	May 17	Sep 22	26.73	35.7
Madison	1079	1939	84	60	20	-1	109	-32	May 7	Sep 26	25.02	41.7
Maple Plain	1030	1898	82	59	19	-1	112	-37	May 7	Oct 5	30.20	55.9
Marshall/Lynd	1151	1902	84	61	21	2	109	-43	May 13	Sep 28	25.33	48.2
Meadowlands	1270	1910	78	52	16	-8	103	-51	June 4	Aug 31	27.62	46.2
Milaca	1080	1902	81	57	17	-3	108	-44	May 12	Sep 25	29.76	37.1
Milan	1005	1893	83	59	18	-3	113	-42	May 15	Sep 25	25.18	37.2
Minneapolis AP	830	1819	83	63	20	2	108	-40	Apr 29	Oct 13	26.36	49.1
Montevideo	900	1889	83	60	19	-1	110	-39	May 7	Oct 1	26.78	34.9
Moorhead-Fargo	940	1881	83	58	14	-5	114	-48	May 12	Sep 28	19.59	35.9
Moose Lake	1085	1939	80	53	17	-7	101	-53	May 24	Sep 13	28.28	36.5
Mora	1001	1904	81	57	18	-4	108	-48	May 14	Sep 21	28.78	41.2
Morris	1130	1885	82	59	16	-3	109	-41	May 12	Sep 25	23.88	35.7
Moscow, Russia	505	1895	76	55	21	9	100	-43	May 8	Sep 26	24.80	63.4
New Hope	905	1956	83	62	20	3	105	-29	May 3	Oct 4	30.95	49.0
New Ulm	826	1864	84	61	21	1	111	-37	May 10	Sep 29	28.02	42.1
North St. Paul	982	1962	83	61	20	2	102	-30	May 2	Oct 11	31.03	54.5
Park Rapids	1434	1885	80	56	15	-8	107	-51	May 21	Sep 20	25.94	51.8
Pembina, ND	780	1872	81	55	9	-11	109	-51	May 25	Sep 17	18.10	37.3
Pigeon River	950	1924	(no temperature readings taken)								32.45	107.4
Pine River Dam	1215	1887	80	56	16	-7	104	-53	May 24	Sep 16	27.31	44.0
Pipestone	1735	1902	84	58	20	-1	108	-40	May 10	Sep 30	24.90	33.1
Pokegama Dam	1280	1887	78	55	15	-7	103	-59	May 30	Sep 11	26.81	49.9
Prior Lake	930	1982	81	61	21	1	104	-36	Apr 25	Oct 2	34.50	64.0
Red Lake Falls	1035	1915	80	56	11	-10	110	-50	May 28	Sep 16	21.07	44.1

*Lowest temperature reported by a ship on western Lake Superior. Lower temperatures have undoubtedly occurred when the lake was frozen—but, of course, when there were no ships out to record them.

STATION	ELEV.	YEAR RECORDS BEGIN	AVERAGE TEMP.				TEMPERATURE EXTREMES		LAST/FIRST FREEZING TEMP.		AVERAGE ANNUAL	
			JULY		JAN.		HIGH	LOW	SPRING	FALL	PRECIP.	SNOW
			MAX.	MIN.	MAX.	MIN.						
Red Lake Indian Agency	1216	1912	78	56	13	-8	109	-50	May 25	Sep 23	22.38	42.9
Red Wing	688	1915	83	62	21	2	106	-41	May 4	Oct 8	29.75	45.0
Redwood Falls AP	1021	1914	84	60	19	-2	110	-33	May 3	Oct 3	24.91	37.0
Rochester AP	1297	1886	81	60	20	2	108	-42	May 8	Sep 28	28.25	47.9
Roseau	1047	1905	78	53	9	-12	107	-52	May 26	Sep 13	20.39	33.5
Roseville	962	1961	83	63	21	4	105	-35	Apr 29	Oct 8	31.44	57.3
St. Cloud AP	1034	1875	82	58	17	-3	107	-42	May 7	Sep 27	27.72	44.0
St. Paul	920	1859	82	62	21	3	107	-41	Apr 30	Oct 9	29.10	43.8
St. Peter	825	1887	84	61	21	1	109	-40	May 9	Sep 30	28.11	34.5
Sandy Lake Dam	1234	1898	78	56	16	-6	102	-52	May 26	Sep 18	27.94	50.7
Sioux Falls AP, SD	1418	1899	86	62	23	2	110	-42	May 5	Oct 3	24.12	39.7
Springfield	1050	1941	84	60	20	1	105	-27	May 6	Oct 7	25.38	39.9
Superior, WI	703	1910	77	53	19	-2	105	-37	May 12	Oct 4	27.87	41.1
Thief River Falls	1130	1911	80	55	11	-10	108	-47	May 25	Sep 17	21.20	33.2
Tracy	1403	1912	84	60	21	1	108	-33	May 7	Oct 4	25.03	46.5
Two Harbors	614	1894	74	52	20	1	99	-36	May 15	Oct 5	28.50	54.2
Virginia	1445	1894	78	53	15	-7	103	-46	May 24	Sep 17	27.09	64.1
Wadena	1350	1918	80	57	15	-6	112	-43	May 17	Sep 20	26.51	48.7
Warroad	1069	1908	77	55	10	-12	103	-55	May 24	Sep 19	20.15	39.5
Waseca	1153	1915	82	59	20	0	106	-37	May 10	Sep 27	30.62	35.7
Wheaton	1018	1916	84	60	18	-2	113	-38	May 10	Sep 25	21.32	37.7
Willmar	1133	1907	82	60	17	-2	107	-38	May 8	Sep 29	27.71	39.2
Windom	1375	1922	84	60	21	1	105	-36	May 17	Sep 29	26.80	38.9
Winnebago	1110	1895	83	60	21	3	107	-35	May 5	Oct 5	30.29	35.2
Winnibigoshish Dam	1315	1887	79	56	14	-8	103	-49	May 21	Sep 27	25.61	49.5
Winona	652	1896	84	61	24	4	108	-40	Apr 29	Oct 8	32.71	38.3
Worthington	1593	1895	83	61	20	1	110	-37	May 7	Oct 5	25.78	39.1
Zumbrota	985	1904	83	59	21	0	109	-45	May 12	Sep 26	29.49	32.0

For those stations that record these things, here are some additional statistics of interest:

Number of Thunderstorms—This is actually the average yearly number of days with thunderstorms. Some days may have two or more thunderstorms, but this doesn't affect the average.

Number of Clear and Cloudy Days—On a clear day, clouds cover three tenths or less of the sky, on the average, from sunrise to sunset. This could mean solid overcast for three hours, then completely clear for the rest of the day, or it could mean scattered puffy clouds all day long.

A cloudy day is one on which eight tenths or more of the sky is covered, on average, between sunup and sundown.

Percent Sunshine—The number here is the percentage of possible sunshine—the monthly number of hours that the sun shines, given as a percentage of the number of hours the sun would have shone had the skies been clear all month. November is the cloudiest month in Minnesota, and July is the sunniest.

Noon Humidity—This is the average relative humidity, in percent, measured at noon in January and July.

Fog—Number of days per year with fog that reduces visibility to one-quarter mile or less.

STATION	NO. OF THUNDER-STORMS	NO. OF DAYS CLEAR	CLOUDY	PERCENT SUNSHINE NOV.	JULY	NOON HUMIDITY JAN.	JULY	DAYS W/ HEAVY FOG
Duluth (AP)	35	76	188	35	65	69	59	54
Duluth (City)	30	115	109	36	68	79	64	43
International Falls	31	78	186		68	57	15	
La Crosse, WI	40	95	173			67	57	21
Moorhead-Fargo	33	88	168	40	71	71	55	13
Minneapolis AP	36	96	168	39	72	66	54	11
Rochester	41	86	182			73	60	34
St. Cloud	36	95	168			69	55	20
St. Paul	34			44	71	73	55	2
Sioux Falls, SD	43	105	157			67	53	22

MINNESOTA'S CHANGING (?) CLIMATE

■■■■■■■■■■■■■■■■■■■■■■■■■■■■■

On Halloween night, 1991, a swath of Minnesota from the Twin Cities to Duluth was buried under 2' to 3' of snow. This was the snowstorm of the century (so far), and it brought normal life to a halt. Now, imagine what it would be like if the snow were a *mile* deep. Don't laugh—it's happened before, and may happen again someday. All it takes is a change of climate.

Is Minnesota's climate changing? Are there cycles of drought and deluge? How's the "greenhouse effect," that feared warming of our planet due to gases released into the atmosphere by factories and fires, coming along? Were winters *really* snowier when your grandmother was a kid? With everyone from grandparents to scientists to congressmen talking about climate change, one starts to get the impression that it really might be happening! This is an interesting and important issue, but before we jump into the question of climate change, it makes sense to describe what climate *is*.

CLIMATE VERSUS WEATHER

Climate is not the same as weather. Weather is the state of the atmosphere—temperature, pressure, wind, cloudiness, where it's raining and where it isn't, the positions of highs, lows, and fronts on the weather map, and many other factors—at any given moment. Weather, of course, is *always* changing!

On the other hand, climate is the overall average of weather over a long period of time. A complete description of the climate is not just a bunch of averages, but also includes a description of the variability of the weather from day to day, from summer to winter, and from year to year. After all, the Twin Cities temperature can stray rather far from its annual average of 45°, and nobody is surprised when one year averages several degrees warmer or colder than the previous year.

So, it's trite but true that nothing is so constant as change, and climatologists recognize this. However, any definition that considers the Great Ice Age, the steamy era of the dinosaurs, and the present as all being part of the same climate isn't very practical (a Minnesota farmer wouldn't know whether to plant bananas or hunt walruses). While one exceptionally hot summer or bitter winter does not mean a change of climate, the melting of Minnesota's two-mile-thick ice sheet 10,000 years ago obviously did.

There must be a happy medium somewhere, and the World Meteorological Organization, along with the National Weather Service and National Oceanographic and Atmospheric Administration, have concurred that averages taken over a 30-year period give the most useful definition of climate. As noted previously, the climate data tables in this book use currently available averages, which cover 1951 through 1980. There's nothing magic about 30 years; many climatologists think 10 years works just as well. In either case the averaging period is long enough to smooth out the large year-to-year fluctuations and reduce the impact of individual extreme years, but not so long as to mask important long-term changes of, say, rainfall patterns. Furthermore, a 10- to 30-year average gives a better guess as to what next year may bring than does a 5-year or 50-year average.

Enough generalities; now let's get specific. Fortunately for Minnesota's climate watchers, the Surgeon General of the U.S. Army, Dr. James Tilton, decided back in 1814 that it would be a good idea for weather records to be taken at the army's remote outposts in the Northwest Territories. One of the most remote stations was established at the confluence of the St. Peter (now the Minnesota) and Mississippi rivers in August 1819. Two months later the post's medical officer began reading his thermometer. In 1825, the post was named Fort Snelling.

The first few years were extremely difficult ones for the isolated soldiers. Mortality from disease and poor diets was high, and the outpost was less than a year old when, in April 1820, it was struck by a tornado! In spite of these hardships the temperatures were faithfully recorded, and this rugged beginning marks the start of one of the most remarkable and useful climate records in the New World. Several eastern cities, such as Philadelphia, Charleston, Cambridge (Massachusetts), and Quebec City, can brag of climate records extending as far back as the 1730s. However, the Fort Snelling weather log, along with subsequent records taken at various locations around the Minneapolis–St. Paul area, comprise *the* longest continuous chronicle of temperature and precipitation in the interior of the North American continent! The importance of this lengthy temperature record extends far beyond the borders of the North Star State, and even has some effect on the answers to such weighty global issues as the greenhouse effect.

To some Minnesotans, especially in winter, the greenhouse effect may not seem like such a bad idea. The basic premise is that the sun heats the earth, and the warm earth radiates its excess heat back into space. The balance between the incoming sunlight and outgoing radiation determines the average temperature of the planet. Certain gases in the atmosphere, notably carbon dioxide, absorb the outgoing radiation and block the escape of heat to space—in much the same manner as does the glass roof of a greenhouse. And as in a greenhouse, the earth warms beneath the blanket of carbon dioxide. We know the greenhouse effect works—just look at the planet Venus. Venus' atmosphere has 260,000 times more carbon dioxide than does earth's, and a typical thermometer reading on Venus is 855° Fahrenheit.

Meanwhile, back on earth, the amount of carbon dioxide in our atmosphere is increasing, thanks to the burning of oil and forests. So far, the increase has been relatively modest, about 20 percent in the past century. Theoretically, the warming over the past century due to carbon dioxide should have been about a degree, plus or minus, with larger rises projected over the next few decades as more carbon dioxide is dumped into the air. Well, that's the theory. Nature doesn't always behave to our expectations, so it's worthwhile to look at the climate and see what the atmosphere itself thinks of global warming. Of course, the 170-year temperature record at Fort Snelling and the Twin Cities is an obvious place to seek to trace the greenhouse effect.

It sounds so simple—just gather together all these old temperature readings, work out their annual mean temperature, plot them on a graph and see if it's getting warmer or colder. There are complications, however. While the exact details are lost to history, the Fort Snelling thermometer was probably mounted on the north wall of a building; nowadays thermometers are placed in ventilated boxes to shield them from direct sunlight. It's possible that in the early spring, as the sun moved higher in the sky but before the trees leafed out, the sun may have struck Fort Snelling's thermometer at certain times of the day, giving a false (too high) temperature reading. Furthermore, for the first 30 years the Fort Snelling readings were taken three times a day, at 7 a.m., 2 p.m. and 9 p.m., and the average of the three was taken to be the daily mean temperature. Since thermometers registering the highest and lowest temperatures of the day became widely available in the late 1800s, the procedure has been to average these high and low readings for the daily mean. The results of the two methods are not always the same, even at the same location on the same day!

Fortunately, once these differences in weather observing techniques are known, they can be taken into consideration to derive an "adjusted" and, we hope, improved temperature record. While all this may sound like mere minutiae, I've mentioned it to show that these mean annual temperatures, be they for Fort Snelling or averages for the world, are not necessarily precise, and to give you something to think about before believing that a 1° climate change is real!

Bruce Watson, of Roseville, kindly provided me with 170 years of Twin Cities area average temperatures based on readings taken at Fort Snelling, Minneapolis, St. Paul and, for the past 100 years, Farmington (about 20 miles south of St. Paul). Watson chose Farmington, rather than some of the other weather stations closer to Fort Snelling, to reduce the "urban warming" effect on temperatures recorded around the Twin Cities. The Farmington record is remarkable in that for over a century the rainfall and temperature have been read daily at the same farmstead by members of the Akin family. No adjustments are needed for these temperatures.

It's worth mentioning that the Akins, along with nearly 200 other weather watchers in Minnesota and thousands more nationwide, have been taking these readings on a volunteer basis. Every month they send a weather summary to the National Climate Data Center in Asheville, North Carolina, where it is used to detail the climate of the United

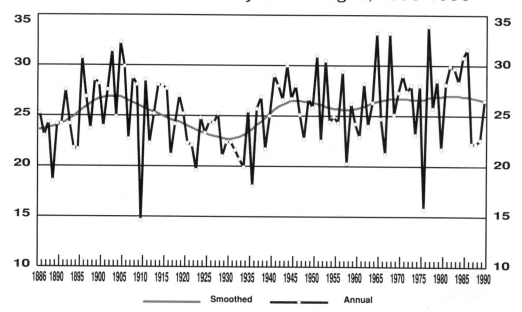

MINNESOTA STATEWIDE AVERAGE PRECIPITATION
Annual values and 20-year averages, 1896-1990

Data from National Oceanographic and Atmospheric Administration © A&WGP

States. There are only five National Weather Service weather stations in Minnesota (Duluth, International Falls, Minneapolis–St. Paul, Rochester, and St. Cloud), so without this commendable effort by citizen weather observers, we would know virtually nothing about the climate of most of Minnesota.

Perhaps the most striking thing about the Twin Cities area annual temperatures is how much they can change from one year to the next! The warmest year, 1931, averaged 11° warmer than 1875, the coldest year, a climate change equivalent to moving 450 miles north or south. The warmest years—1931, 1846, 1878 and 1987—are pretty well scattered throughout the 170-year record, while the coldest years—1875, 1843, 1883 and 1867— were all more than 100 years ago. Remarkable temperature swings occurred during 1843-1847 and 1875-1879, when annual temperatures steadily rose by 9° over three years, then plummeted back to normal levels after the fourth year. The lesson here is to be wary of thinking that several warm (or cold) years mean a real trend! Speaking of trends, the smooth, curving line shows a running 30-year average of annual temperatures—essentially, a year-by-year account of the changing climate.

Overall, there is a slight increase in the temperature, with the 1990 "normal" being about a degree higher than the 1820 "normal." However, the warming trend is not a steady one, and 1° dips occurred around the Civil War and again in the 1960s. For mathematical reasons, each 30-year average is only accurate to only about half a degree, leading to the possibility that the 1° warming over 170 years is just a statistical fluke! There's also the possibility that the increase, if real, is due to the urban warming of the Twin Cities "heat

island" extending out to Farmington (statewide average temperatures, calculated by averaging all the weather stations in Minnesota, show *no* warming since 1895). So, is Minnesota's climate changing for the warmer? I don't think anybody can say for sure right now.

There's more to climate than simple averages. Personally, I think extremes are more
interesting than averages, and what could be more extreme than the highest and lowest
temperatures recorded anywhere in the state each year? If you're wondering whether
summers are growing hotter or if winters are getting colder, a peek at the extreme temperatures might give you a clue. Just keep in mind that a single heat wave or cold snap doesn't
always mean an exceptional summer or winter. Prior to 1886 there weren't enough weather
stations in Minnesota to provide meaningful statewide extremes; the yearly highs and lows
since then show no distinct trends to hotter hots or colder colds, nor is there any clear-cut
moderation in the extremes. There are, however, two outstanding stretches of extreme
weather: a long spell of hot summers from 1930 through 1941, when some place in the
state exceeded 105° every year, and a nearly as long stretch of bitter winters between 1895
and 1904, during which the state's all-time low of 59 below zero was recorded—twice!
Minnesota's all-time high of 114.5° came in 1917, a year that was, on the average, Minnesota's and the Twin Cities' coldest year of the past century! Meanwhile, in 1933 and
1936, at the height of the hot summers, winter temperatures plummeted to 55 below zero,
readings that haven't been equaled since.

The 169° *range* of temperatures in 1936, from 55 below to 114 above, was the greatest in Minnesota's history. Meanwhile, the *average* temperatures for both 1933 and 1936
were very close to normal, masking the incredible variety that occurred each year!

To many, including most farmers, rainfall is more important than temperature. Minnesota's weirdest and most devastating climate fluke, the Dust Bowl years of the 1930s, was
due much more to a rainfall shortage than to the extreme temperatures of the decade.

MINNESOTA YEARLY EXTREME TEMPERATURES
Highest and lowest in state each year, 1886-1900

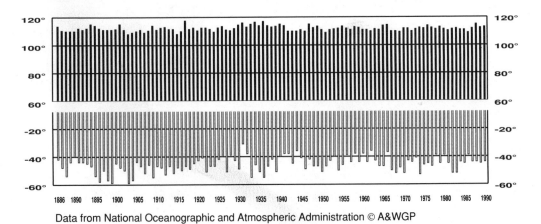

Data from National Oceanographic and Atmospheric Administration © A&WGP

However, rainfall records are lot more volatile than temperature records. A single downpour at Fort Snelling, or anywhere else, could push its annual precipitation way above normal, while drought reigns generally throughout the state. For example: in July 1987, Minneapolis–St. Paul Airport was deluged by 10" of rain in one day, pushing the Twin City yearly total to 32". That's 6" more than normal. However, that storm missed most of Minnesota, and the statewide average precipitation of 22" was nearly 4" *below* the long-term average. So let's look at the 105-year-long record of statewide precipitation, averaged over many rainfall reporting stations all across Minnesota.

As with temperature, the statewide average precipitation shows its greatest variability from year to year, with the longer-term trends changing more sedately. The two driest years—1910 and 1976—were each followed by wet years with twice as much precipitation; indeed, 1976, the second driest year, was followed by the *wettest* year! In both cases the rapid return to rainy conditions kept the droughts from becoming very severe.

The multi-year dry spells from 1929 through 1936 and 1987 through 1989 resulted in the worst droughts of the century, even though neither period had exceptionally dry individual years (also, dry summers produce more severe droughts than do dry winters, so overall annual precipitation is not always the best indicator of drought).

On the longer view, there doesn't seem to be any general increase or decrease in precipitation over the past 105 years. What does stand out in the record are two protracted dry spells—from the beginning of the record in 1886 until 1895, and from 1921 to 1939. Both dry spells resulted in pronounced dips in the long-term trend of precipitation. Longer records from Fort Snelling and the Twin Cities area indicate that the first dry spell began around 1882, and that there was an even earlier dry period from the 1830s until the late 1850s (however, these records are based on one or two rain gauges, not a statewide network). Severe as it was, the 1987-1989 drought failed to bring down the long-term trend.

Talk of droughts inevitably leads to talk of cycles, and particularly of the 22-year "sunspot cycle." Sunspots are, essentially, storms on the sun, which is a long way from Minnesota. However, the sun drives the earth's weather in the first place. The uneven heating of the planet, more in the tropics and less in the arctic, and the need for the atmosphere to balance this inequality by sending warm air to the poles and cold air back to the tropics, are the ultimate causes of wind and weather. So, the wind blows because the sun shines, and it seems plausible that any changes on the sun might affect the weather on earth.

Exactly how this might happen is another question, but statistically, the climate record shows some evidence of a 22-year cycle of droughts in the Great Plains. Minnesota is on the fringes of the Great Plains, but nonetheless the occurrence of drought years—1889, 1910, 1934, 1954 and 1976—shows a roughly 22-year spacing. Mind you, the cycle is far from perfect, since, for example, 1954 was not a severe drought year in Minnesota, while the much worse drought of 1988 fails to fit into the pattern.

On the average, the years around the bottom of the 22-year cycle receive about 10 percent less precipitation and the years around the peak of the cycle. That's not much of a difference, considering that it's common for one year to have 50 percent more (or less) precipitation than the next year. Anyway, those are the facts; I'll let you decide if sunspots really cause droughts.

Now, to the ultimate question about climate change, and it's a question that has torn families apart. Were winters *really* snowier when your grandmother (or mother) was a kid? Sorry, Grandma, but the answer, according to 130 years of snowfall records at Minneapolis and St. Paul, is no. At both cities, six of the 10 snowiest winters occurred between 1961 and 1984. At Minneapolis, the two snowiest winters of record were 1981-1982 and 1983-1984. In Grandma's favor, though, it should be noted that these recent snowy winters were recorded at the airport, and that airport snowfalls are not entirely comparable to city records. First of all, the city has a warming effect that reduces accumulated snowfall, and second, airport weather observers, who are on duty 24 hours a day, tend to be a bit more diligent about measuring snow than are observers at part-time weather stations. But then again, at the St. Paul weather station, which is still in the city, recent winters have been every bit as snowy as at the Minneapolis airport. Up north, at International Falls and Duluth, the second half of this century has been snowier than the first half, but both of those weather stations have moved to airports, too.

You might have noticed that I keep coming back to a basic problem with climate data: the inaccuracies and inconsistencies in weather measurements over the years, and that the resulting errors in climate statistics may be as large as actual climate changes. It's a real quandary for climatologists, since there's intense interest from many sides—government agencies, the media, industry and agriculture, and the public—in definite yes or no answers to questions like the greenhouse effect. Unfortunately, the odds are that simple yes or no answers won't be available until we have more years of more accurate climate observations, or the greenhouse effect becomes unmistakably large.

Enough of these mere hiccups in the earth's climate. Let's talk about the granddaddy of them all—the Great Ice Age. No worry about inaccurate thermometers and half-degree temperature differences here; the evidence is literally carved in stone all across Minnesota. On a steamy August afternoon it might seem inconceivable that only 18,000 years earlier (a mere blink of an eye, geologically speaking), most of Minnesota was buried under one or two miles of solid ice (in January it might seem a little more believable). Other ice sheets covered northern Europe, from Britain to Russia, and Antarctica.

The greatest ice sheet of all time formed around Hudson's Bay and spread across half of North America. Sheets of glacier ice extended as far south as Saint Louis, Missouri, with the Ohio and Missouri rivers marking the southernmost boundaries of the ice sheet. The basins that are now the Great Lakes were scoured out by the glaciers' plowing action, and the rocky debris was deposited in huge gravel banks all across Minnesota. For unknown reasons (possibly the blocking effect of the northern Wisconsin highlands), extreme southeastern Minnesota, along with parts of southern Wisconsin, escaped the icy onslaught.

Apparently there were many ice ages—various counts range from four or five to 20 or more. The whole mess started about 2 million years ago, and the ice has advanced and retreated every 100,000 years or so ever since. It's hard to tell how many of the glacial advances reached Minnesota, since each one effectively erased the geological evidence of the previous glaciers. Between each of these ice ages the climate was much like it is today. The last round began 80,000 or 90,000 years ago, and the ice sheets reached their maximum size 18,000 years ago (or 16,000 B.C.). Around 12,000 B.C. the world's climate suddenly warmed up to near present temperatures, and the Big Melt began. Minnesota's last glacial ice disappeared around 10,000 B.C. It took another 5,000 years to melt the rest of the huge mass of ice, and the last patch disappeared from northern Quebec around 5,000 B.C. The ice age is still on in Antarctica and Greenland, and remnant ice caps remain on some islands of northeastern Canada.

Today's Minnesota landscape is littered with geological relics from the Ice Age. Exposed rocks along the shores of northeastern Minnesota's lakes, including Superior, show the smooth, striated polishing action of the moving ice. Moraines, those piles of left-over gravel, cover much of southwestern Minnesota. Chunks of ice left in the gravel by the retreating glaciers melted into water-filled depressions called "kettle ponds," while rocks left by melt water in glacial crevasses became long, gravelly ridges known as "eskers."

The levels of lakes Duluth and Houghton, predecessors to today's Lake Superior, changed drastically as the glaciers came and went. Along Duluth's Skyline Drive, 500 feet above the waters of Lake Superior, the ancient beaches of Lake Duluth still can be seen. Other stranded beaches from Lake Agassiz, which filled the Red River basin, lie near Ada in northwestern Minnesota. Meanwhile, the glacier-free terrain around Winona, with its rolling hills and ravines, looks more like Kentucky or Missouri (which also escaped the ice) than the rest of Minnesota.

Needless to say, Minnesota's ice-age climate was quite different from today's. Exactly how different is a matter of some speculation, but combining geologic clues with some logical deductions based on modern meteorology, we can guess what it was like. Obviously, it was cold—especially when the land was buried in ice. It was probably also quite windy, since the temperature difference between the Arctic and the tropics was larger, and that's what drives the wind. There's also geologic evidence for wind—deep deposits of dust, known as "loess," blown onto southern Minnesota from the arid plains to the west. With so much water locked up in the ice sheets, the world's oceans were 300 feet shallower than they are today, and Minnesota's prime source of moisture—the Gulf of Mexico—was much smaller and cooler. Thus, Minnesota was probably a lot drier during the Ice Age.

That's what happened; now the question is: Why? There are many theories explaining the ice ages, and some of them may actually be true. One plausible idea put forth in 1920 by a Yugoslavian named Milankovitch concerns the wobbles of the earth and its orbit. Like a spinning top, the axis of earth's poles wobbles around and changes its tilt in cycles of 26,000 and 40,000 years, while the shape of the earth's orbit around the sun changes over several longer cycles—up to 100,000 years. The actual size of the orbit never changes, and, over an entire year, the total amount of sunlight reaching the earth never changes. However, the wobbles vary the amount of sunlight reaching the different hemispheres during different seasons by 5 or 10 percent over thousands of years. When the northern hemisphere gets less summer sunlight, that season is cooler. As it is now, the winter snows that cover the far north barely melt before summer is over; if summers were 5° cooler, the snow might not melt at all. New snow would fall on the old, and the snow layer would build up year after year. When the snow gets deep enough it increases the cooling by reflecting sunlight back into space. Keep that up for a few thousand years and there's an ice sheet.

The Milankovitch theory predicts several possible ice-age cycles, and some of them are close to the observed 100,000-year (plus or minus) cycle. The theory also predicts that the past ice age was not the last one, and that the next one could start in 5,000 or 10,000 years. That raises the possibility of a titanic duel between the Milankovitch and greenhouse effects, with the stakes being a climate that ends in either fire or ice. Stay tuned!

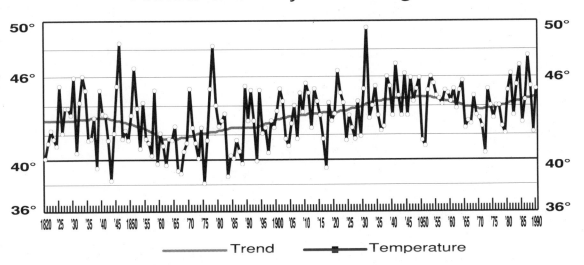

MINNEAPOLIS-ST. PAUL AREA AVERAGE
ANNUAL TEMPERATURE
Annual and 30-year averages

Data from Bruce Watson © A&WGP

THE DAY THE SUN DIED

■■■■■■■■■■■■■■■■■■■■■■■■■■■■

The sun rises awfully early in Minnesota at the end of June, and usually only the milkman pays it much attention. However, the sunrise on Wednesday, June 30, 1954, was not your ordinary sunrise. For one, the sun rose not as a brilliant red ball, but as a shining crescent that looked more like a celestial fingernail clipping. Even more exceptional, however, were the crowds—thousands upon thousands of Minnesotans, from school children and their parents and grandparents, to reporters and photographers, and even astronomers (for whom sunrise normally marks the end of the work day), crowding rooftops and bridges to catch a view of the rising sun. The crescent thinned to a sliver as the sun cleared the horizon, and at 5:07 a.m.—27 minutes after sunrise—the sun disappeared completely.

The occasion was, of course, the greatest show not-quite-on-earth, a total eclipse of the sun. The earth catches an average of 70 total eclipses per century, but their narrow paths delight in crossing oceans, jungles and deserts, leaving the populated world to read about the fortunate few who get to see the spectacle. On the average, any given spot on the planet sees a total eclipse only once every 400 years. Most humans never see one. Minnesotans have managed to beat those odds a little—a total eclipse on August 7, 1869, darkened the southwestern corner of the state, and on January 24, 1925, a dawn eclipse was seen from International Falls, Cass Lake, Cusson, Marble, and other North Woods communities, although clouds obscured the view from Duluth.

In many respects, the 1954 eclipse was kinder than most. Rather than avoiding populated places, the 70-mile-wide path of totality passed directly over the Minneapolis–St. Paul metropolitan area. Forty seconds earlier the moon's long, tapered shadow first touched the earth near O'Neill, Nebraska, and swept quickly northeastward across southern Minnesota into northern Wisconsin and Michigan. After leaving North America at the coast of Labrador, the moon's shadow crossed the North Atlantic to Scandinavia. Thousands more saw the eclipse through partly cloudy skies in southern Norway and Sweden (never in history, perhaps, had more Swedes and Norwegians on both sides of the Atlantic had a chance to see the same total solar eclipse!), and less than three hours after the sunrise spectacle in Minnesota, the lunar shadow departed the earth near Jodhpur, India, where the eclipse was seen at sunset.

Minneapolis Star *photographer Roy Swan shot this sequence of the 1954 eclipse from the roof of a hotel across from Loring Park. Sun images were recorded with a stationary camera at seven-minute intervals beginning at 4:54 a.m.*

The weather was also kind. Would-be eclipse watchers wince at the thought of a once-in-four-or-five-lifetimes event being skunked by clouds, but a cold front crossed the state the day before, and Minnesotans had sparkling clear skies on eclipse morning. The eclipse it-self had a small effect on the weather. Members of the Junior Astronomy Club of Minne-apolis recorded a temperature drop of one degree, from 62° to 61°, as the eclipse progressed.

It's tempting to report stories of all activity in the Twin Cities grinding to a halt as the sun flickered out, but the truth is that at 5:07 a.m. there wasn't much activity to halt. The cities, normally sleepy at that hour, actually came to life for the event. Northern States Power reported a 9 percent increase in electricity use, indicating that 50,000 normally somnolent households were up and about. At the Minneapolis airport, fifty passengers boarded a spe-cial Northwest Airlines "Stratocruiser" flight at 3:50 a.m. to view the eclipse from 20,000 feet above Lake Minnetonka. Millions of television viewers across the nation watched the eclipse broadcast live from the University of Minnesota observatory in Minneapolis.

The eclipse itself is perhaps best described by an excerpt from an article the next day's *Minneapolis Tribune,* titled "The Day the Sun Died": "All at once, the spectacle changed, and the 'show' set atingle a primal nerve deep in every viewer. As the sun winked out and watchers dropped their eye shields, they noticed the weirdly-lit landscape. They noticed a broad track of dusk marching across the sky. For a moment, science was blacked out and it was dark—as dark as the Dark Ages. The most warmly-clad spectator shivered then, as he looked at a world transformed by a light that was not light, and gloom that was not darkness. Then, as suddenly, the dark disk in the sky sparkled at the upper edge and the spell was cast off as warm light returned to earth." The total eclipse lasted 76 seconds. The next one, at 10:45 a.m. September 14, 2099, will bring over 4 minutes of totality to central Min-nesota, and another eclipse at 1:36 p.m. on May 3, 2106, will last 3 minutes, 46 seconds. Weather permitting, the Twin Cities will see both eclipses.

THE AURORA: NIGHT LIGHTS OF THE NORTH COUNTRY

■ ■

There are many ways to spend a clear night; one of the finest is to watch the aurora borealis, or northern lights. This is particularly true in Minnesota, where auroras are fairly frequent, and especially during the winter, when the otherwise long and dark nights might seem to have little else to offer. However, the northern lights are a delight any time of year— watch one reflecting off the still waters of a lake while loons provide background music and you'll know what I mean!

Displays of the aurora often begin as a pale green arch hugging the northern horizon, and many nights the show never progresses beyond this stage. Some nights, though, "search-light beams" grow out of the glow and criss-cross the sky, multiplying and merging into red and green curtains that march overhead and off to the south. At times, the entire sky may shine and shimmer like an incongruous mixture of fire and Jello.

Of course, we know the aurora is neither fire nor Jello, but for centuries the actual cause of these lights was a complete mystery. The word "aurora" means "dawn" in Latin and "borealis" means north; Down Under, the southern-hemisphere equivalent is the "aurora australis." Since the days of Aristotle in ancient Greece the most acceptable explanations of the "northern dawn" involved peculiar kinds of twilight—for example, sunlight reflect-ing off the polar ice back into the sky. Auroras were also blamed on distant forest fires il-luminating the sky, or even spontaneous combustion of the air itself. It wasn't until the beginning of this century, when the first rudiments of atomic physics were being worked out, that the true cause of the aurora came to light.

Auroras work on the same basic principle as fluorescent or neon lights, or outdoor mercury and sodium vapor lamps. The gas—neon, mercury or sodium—glows when en-ergetic, high speed electrons are run through it. In the case of the aurora, the gases are mostly oxygen and nitrogen (the main constituents of air). High speed electrons strike the gas molecules, jolting the molecules' electrons out of their tiny orbits. When the molecu-lar electrons drop back to their original orbits, they lose the energy they picked up from the high speed electrons. This energy radiates away as light.

The high speed electrons in fluorescent lights come from the house current, with an extra kick given by the lamp's ballast mechanism. The aurora is lit by electrons from the sun, which need no boost. Electrons thrown out by hot spots in the solar atmosphere known as solar flares can travel the 93 million miles to earth in less than a day. The solar electrons zip along at 1,000 miles per second for most of their journey, but several thousand miles short of earth they get caught in our planet's magnetic field. This magnetic field has broad loops connecting the north and south poles, just like the familiar pattern around a bar magnet. The electrons are deflected north or south along these loops, dipping down into the atmosphere as they approach the poles. To an electron, the magnetic field looks somewhat like an apple, with electrons on the surface of the apple moving "north" or "south" into one of the dimples. The electrons are finally funneled into the top of the atmosphere in a ring (called the "auroral oval") surrounding each of the magnetic poles.

Electrons are always funneling down to earth, and there's always an aurora—albeit faint most of the time—along the auroral oval. But the extremely energetic electrons shot from solar flares penetrate much deeper into the magnetic field before getting caught. Their trajectories bring them into the atmosphere farther from the poles, the (northern) auroral oval expands south, and Minnesotans see the northern lights.

The same electrons that create such beauty in the sky can wreak havoc on earth. Disturbances in the earth's magnetic field brought on by all this electricity can induce electrical currents in long metal objects such as telephone wires, power lines and pipelines, leading to power outages and communications disruptions. A "magnetic storm" in 1989 knocked out the power grid for the entire province of Quebec. Long-distance radio communications may be wiped out as electrons alter the upper atmosphere's ability to reflect radio waves at certain frequencies (particularly shortwave). It has even been suggested that solar disturbances may trigger storm development and influence droughts, but these theories are quite controversial among meteorologists.

The aurora gives us a chance to glimpse the very highest reaches of our atmosphere. Most auroras shine between 60 and 200 miles up, but occasionally a really big show can reach as high as 600 miles—higher than most satellites! In contrast to these enormous vertical dimensions, the curtains themselves are only a few thousand feet thick. Often the curtains shade from greenish on the bottom to red at the top; both colors come from oxygen atoms. Occasionally a deep violet glow from nitrogen atoms appears in the higher reaches of the aurora.

The north and south poles of earth's magnet—the dimples on the apple, so to speak—are not exactly at the geographic north and south poles, but about 1,000 miles away. That places the magnetic north pole over Ellesmere Island in the Canadian Arctic. This quirk of our magnetic field is a boon for Minnesota aurora watchers, since it brings the magnetic north pole—and the auroral oval—1,000 miles closer, increasing the frequency of auroras. At the same geographic latitudes in Asia auroras are much less frequent than they are in North America.

Over North America the auroral oval usually runs from northern Alaska, across the northern Northwest Territories, into northern Quebec and Labrador. That's the place to go if you want to see the aurora almost every clear night. Farther south the frequency drops off—to 30 nights a year in northern Minnesota, and about half that for southern Minnesota. Ambitious aurora watchers far from city lights may be able to see even more than these statistics indicate—from Glen Ullin, North Dakota, Jay Brausch spots auroras on an average of 85 nights a year! The southernmost aurora borealis on record was seen from the Cayman Islands (19° north latitude) in the Caribbean in March, 1989.

The very name "northern lights" associates auroras with cold places and long nights, and it might seem that they should be most frequent in winter. The truth is, however, that solar flares care little about seasons on earth, and auroras can occur at any time of year. There is actually a clustering of auroras during the equinoctial months of March, April, September, and October. Much more important than any seasonal variability is the effect of the "sunspot cycle", an 11-year cycle of solar activity (including solar flares). While some not very spectacular auroras may be seen throughout the sunspot cycle, the most stunning ones generally reserve themselves for the years right around the peak of the cycle. The last peak was in 1989, when several spectacular shows lit up the skies; the next peak should arrive around 2000.

MINNESOTA WEATHER EVENTS

■■■■■■■■■■■■■■■■■■■■■■■■■■■■

1819   The Army begins weather observations at Fort Snelling in October.

1820   On April 18, a tornado strikes the camp that was soon to become Fort Snelling, damaging the roof of a barracks but, fortunately, injuring no one. It was the first tornado ever reported in Minnesota, and happened to strike the only frame structures in the territory!

1833   The Leonid meteor shower, appearing to emanate from the constellation Leo, shows up every year around November 14. This year the shower put on an exceptional display, with hundreds of meteors per second observed all night at Fort Snelling. There could be a repeat on or about November 17, 1999.

1838   At 2 a.m on February 13 the mercury in the thermometer at Fort Snelling stood, frozen, at -40°. Being frozen, the mercury could sink no lower. However, the temperature could, and the actual cold is unknown.

1843   February and March were two of the coldest months in Twin Cities area history. Fort Snelling's temperature remained below freezing every day of both months, and March's average temperature of 3.0° was 9° lower than that of any March before or since. All this followed an exceptionally mild January.

1855-56   A cold wave arriving on December 22 ushered in one of the coldest winters of record. Except for a few hours on January 1 and 2, the mercury at Fort Ripley stayed at or below zero for the next 20 days, with many afternoon readings in the -10° to -20° range.

1857   The second bitter winter in a row. January's average temperatures were 6.5° below zero at Fort Ripley, and 4.5° below at Fort Snelling. The cold continued into February—on the 10th the Fort Ripley weather observer noted "Thermometer at -50 at 6 a.m. Mercury frozen in charcoal cup. Spirit thermometer at Little Falls 16 miles from the fort - 56 at 6 a.m. The lowest degree of cold on records in the Territory." It was the coldest April ever in the Twin Cities, averaging a mere 31° at Ft. Snelling.

1863   Frost on the ground was reported within 25 miles of St. Paul on July 11, and frost was seen within the city on August 29. On September 18 a trace of snow fell at St. Paul.

1864   On the evening of December 30, 1863, St. Paul's thermometer dropped below zero, where it remained for 226 hours. On New Year's Day the afternoon reading at St. Paul was 25° below zero with a brisk wind! As consolation, the rest of the winter was relatively mild.

1866   Minnesota's "Greatest Blizzard," according to some because of its awesome combination of snow, wind and cold, struck on the night of February 13 and raged for three days. Barns were buried in drifts, and St. Paul's temperature fell to -29° at the end of the blizzard. Unlike some more recent storms, this one struck at night, when most folks were safely home, and human losses were light.

1867   The Chippewa and Pomme de Terre valleys turned into "one broad sheet of water as far as the eye could reach" as a heavy and continuous downpour soaked Pope, Douglas, and Stearns counties on July 18. Barrels empty before the rain were full of water afterwards, and residents of Sauk Centre and Osakis claimed that 30" to 36" of rain fell in as many hours. Frost nipped St. Paul on September 1.

1869   Clear skies made for great viewing of a total solar eclipse on August 7 across extreme southwestern Minnesota.

1870   The world's first "blizzard" hit Iowa and Minnesota on March 14-16, dumping up to 16" of snow. The Estherville (Iowa) *Vindicator* used the boxing term, meaning a volley of punches, to describe the storm. It was the first known use of "blizzard" for this purpose. The name stuck.

1872   A chilly Christmas Eve in Minneapolis, with the mercury struggling to reach -17° at 2 p.m. after a morning low of -38°.

1873   In the middle of a mild afternoon that lured thousands of people out into the forests, fields and towns, a wall of white swept across the Minnesota prairies. Thus commenced the deadly blizzard of January 7-10. Visibility in the blowing snow was reduced to three feet, and cows suffocated in the drifts. More than 70 Minnesotans perished in the sudden onslaught, with many of the dead not discovered until spring. Trains were stuck in drifts for days afterwards. The high death toll resulted from the daytime arrival of the storm—much like the blizzard of 1888 and the Armistice Day Storm of 1940, and unlike the harsher blizzard of 1866.

1875   January and February averaged -3.7° and -2.7°, respectively, at St. Paul, making it the coldest winter ever. The mercury fell to zero or lower on 68 days from November through March, and never rose above freezing from December 19, 1874, through March 8. Along the border with North Dakota, Breckenridge stayed continuously below zero from January 2 through 20.

1876   An icy summer on Lake Superior. At Duluth "the ice extended out as far as the eye can reach, but boats passed in and out." The date—July 3! Most of the ice cleared out that night, but enough remained on the Fourth of July for Duluthians to make ice cream from the last of the lake ice. On December 8, the term blizzard gained official acceptance by appearing in the Weather Bureau publication, *Monthly Weather Review*.

1877   The mildest February on record averaged 31.8° at St. Paul, 16° above normal.

1878   The "Year Without a Winter" across the northern Plains, Midwest and Northeast. St. Paul's temperature for December 1877 through March 1878 averaged 15° above normal, giving Minnesota a Missouri-like winter. The mercury fell to zero only four times during the winter, all in January. Lake Minnetonka's ice cleared out by March 11.

1879   A tornado on July 2 left 14 dead along its path from Minnesota, across the Mississippi River, to Wisconsin. A Christmas cold wave saw temperatures tumble to -58° at St. Vincent in extreme northwestern Minnesota (only 1° shy of the state's all-time low) and -39° at St. Paul (the Twin Cities' lowest December reading ever).

1880   The winter of 1880-1881 got off to an early start with a blizzard on October 16. Some drifts survived until the following spring. That was followed by the Twin Cities' coldest November in 170 years of record, and a severe late December cold wave (-27° at Minneapolis and St. Paul).

1881   It may have been the snowiest winter in St. Paul's history, but, unfortunately, nobody took consistent measurements of the white stuff. The Army Signal Corps did record 35" of accumulation on the ground at the end of January. It definitely was the wettest winter ever, with 13.57" of water (mostly melted snow) from November 1, 1880, through March 31. The spring snow melt brought flooding along the Mississippi and Red rivers, considered the greatest since 1844. A September gale brought 75 m.p.h. sustained winds to Duluth, destroying a lighthouse at the harbor entrance and damaging other port facilities.

1883   The Rochester tornado of August 21 killed 31 residents and injured 100 more. Some died as trains were tossed from the tracks. The silver lining to this gray funnel cloud was that the disaster led to the formation of the world-renowned Mayo Clinic.

1884   A tornado swept from White Bear Lake into Wisconsin, killing 9 and wreaking $4 million in damage—a tremendous sum in those days.

1885   Duluth dropped to its all-time low of 41° below zero on January 2. Fargo-Moorhead had its latest spring freeze (June 8) and earliest autumn freeze (August 25) ever, leaving the area with its shortest summer.

1886   Minnesota's most lethal tornado left 74 dead in Sauk Rapids and St. Cloud on April 14. Among the wreckage were a school, two churches, the Sauk Rapids Post Office, and a bridge.

1887   Rochester has never been so cold, before or since, as it was on January 7 when the thermometer read 4° below.

1888   The legendary "Blizzard of '88" ravaged the Great Plains on January 12-13. Like the 1873 blizzard, the storm struck after a mild morning, trapping many out in the fields and on the road. Many of the 200 deaths were children frozen on their way home from school. At the end of the storm the mercury at St. Paul stood at -37°. The following week another cold wave sent St. Paul's thermometer to its all-time record low of -41°. (In March another "Blizzard of '88" buried New York City and parts of New England, and the two storms should not be confused!)

1889   Only 14" of snow fell on St. Paul during the entire winter of 1888-89, the least snowy winter ever in the Twin Cities. Forest fires raged across northeastern Minnesota into northwestern Wisconsin on June 12-13.

1890   On July 13 a tornado left six dead near St. Paul, while high thunderstorm winds capsized the *Sea Wing* cruising on Lake Pepin, drowning half of the 200 on board.

1892   Blizzard conditions whipped Minnesota on March 8-9, with winds peaking at 70 m.p.h. at Easton. At the end of the storm Duluthians could step out of second-story windows onto snow drifts piled by 60 m.p.h. winds. Minneapolis measured 7.80" of rain on July 26-27, the city's greatest 24-hour rainfall of record—until 1987.

1893   The thermometer lost 40° in five hours at Park Rapids on January 31 as yet another blizzard rolled into Minnesota.

1894   An extremely wet spring as St. Paul and Duluth received twice their normal March through May allotment of precipitation. It was Duluth's wettest spring ever. The soggy spring was followed by a desiccating summer. St. Paul's June-July-August rain total was a mere 2", 9" below normal and the driest on record. Duluth's 3.80" of rain was less than a third of normal. It was a hot summer, too, averaging 4° warmer than normal at St. Paul and Duluth. In late July temperatures as high as 110° coupled with 50 m.p.h. winds to turn the fields and forests into tinderboxes.

Prairie and forest fires broke out across the state in August, sending palls of smoke to the Atlantic. The tinderbox exploded on September 1, when a fire broke out near Mille Lacs Lake and spread east. The ensuing firestorm incinerated the towns of Hinckley and Sandstone along with 500 square miles of forest. At least 418 people, and possibly 100 or 200

The High Bridge over the Mississippi was destroyed when tornadoes struck downtown St. Paul and downtown Minneapolis on August 20, 1904.

more, were consumed in the holocaust. Smoke from the fires halted shipping on Lake Superior, and drifted out across the Atlantic.

1895 Winds of 50 m.p.h. on October 18-20 raised a "sand blizzard" and spread fires across western Minnesota's prairies.

1896 The year started cold at International Falls, where an all-time low of -49° was recorded on January 4. November was cold, too, with the temperature plunging to -45° at Pokegama Dam. A blizzard raged over the Thanksgiving Day holiday. Most towns had their coldest November ever.

1899 The "greatest arctic outbreak in American history" sent the thermometer to 59° below zero at Leech Lake on February 9, an all-time low record for Minnesota. The misery was shared by many—still-standing all-time cold records were set from Montana to Florida to Pennsylvania. The misery was also short-lived—a week after the record cold, Leech Lake had rebounded to 45° above, a gain of 104°.

1900 The re-invigorated remnants of the disastrous Galveston hurricane dropped 6.65" of rain on St. Paul, September 9-11.

1903 The mercury plummeted to -59° at Pokegama Dam on February 16, equalling the state's all-time low set four years earlier. However, the low reading is suspect because the thermometer may have been too close to the ground (where it's normally colder at night). A mid-summer's night freeze occurred at Leech Lake Dam, where the temperature dipped to 26° on July 11.

1904 Downtowns are not immune from tornadoes—the centers of both Minneapolis and St. Paul were both struck by tornadoes on August 20. The St. Paul Weather Bureau office at 4th and Roberts recorded a sustained (1-minute average) wind of 110 m.p.h. as the tornado passed by. A few blocks away the High Bridge over the Mississippi was blown down. Other tornadoes damaged a swath from Glencoe to Stillwater.

1905 In terms of losses, it was Lake Superior's worst shipping year ever—22 ships sunk or damaged beyond repair with a total loss of more than 30 lives. Severe storms struck on August 31 and October 20, but the most memorable was the November 27-28 *"Mataafa* storm." At Duluth winds averaged 60 m.p.h. or greater for 13 hours as the temperature fell from 31° at noon to -10° at midnight on the 27th, and 7" of snow fell. Trying to beat the expiration of its insurance on November 30, the *Mataafa* left Duluth but, heading directly into the gale, made it no further than Two Harbors. The ship struck a pier while trying to re-enter Duluth harbor, was beached just north of the harbor entrance, and broke in two. Nine of the *Mataafa's* 23 sailors drowned.

1907 The chilliest May in the Twin Cities' 170-year-long meteorological history followed cold on the heels of the third coldest April. June was also colder than normal, making it the dreariest April through June on record.

1909 An early snowstorm on October 11-12 was followed by temperatures as low as 7° in northern Minnesota.

1910 Most Minnesota towns had their warmest March ever, and the mercury soared to 88° at Montevideo. It was also one of the driest Marches, with several places receiving no measurable precipitation. The year was the driest of record at Duluth, Minneapolis, St. Paul, Rochester, St. Cloud, and statewide (14.65"). Five-pound hailstones reportedly fell in Todd and Wadena counties on July 27.

1911   A wet year statewide. St. Paul's total precipitation was four times the previous year's meager total. Between the two years, precipitation averaged just about normal.

1912   Averaged over the entire month and across the entire state, January was the coldest month in 95 years of record (1895-1990). The average—8.3° below zero!

1913   One of the most horrendous Great Lakes storms in history swept all five lakes on November 9-10. Three ships sank on Lake Superior, and Duluth recorded 62 m.p.h. winds. (On Lake Huron, eight vessels were lost along with 200 lives.)

1914   A 1.5-mile-wide tornado cut across Grant and Stevens counties on August 16, killing 2 people.

1915   Frosts were seen in northern Minnesota in both July and August.

1916   St. Paul's earliest snow ever fell on September 15. An early blizzard struck on October 19-20, dumping as much as 15" of snow. Temperatures fell 50° or more in the storm—from the 60s on to the 18th to as low as 2° above at Hallock on 20th.

1917   Statewide, it was the coldest year of the century (at least through 1990), with an annual average temperature of 36.5°. And yet, on July 29 Beardsley recorded 114.5°, the state's all-time record high! March was Duluth's snowiest month ever with 48.2", of

Almost all the front page news for October 18, 1918 in the Carlton County Vidette *related to what the paper called a "hurricane of flame and burning leaves and smoke."*

which 21" fell in 24 hours on March 13-14. Duluth also had a chilly summer. Its frost-free season was the shortest ever (87 days), running from June 14 to September 10 (normal frost-free season is 143 days). On June 6, 15 boats were stuck in the ice off Duluth harbor. On September 3 an earthquake rattled a 150- to 200-mile-wide area from Staples to Brainerd.

1918 On the night of August 21 (the 35th anniversary of the Rochester Tornado), a twister wiped out the center of Tyler, leaving 36 dead. The cool, dry and breezy September and October that followed set the stage for an even greater disaster—the fires of October 12.

What a local newspaper called "the awfullest fire horror in state's history" was actually several major fires that scorched 1,500 square miles, the towns of Cloquet, Moose Lake and Brookston, 10,455 houses and barns, 41 schools. At least 453, and possibly 1,000, people died in the flames, 3,000 were injured, and 11,382 were left homeless. Damage totaled $30 million, according to the state Relief Commission, and $70 million according to claims filed by those affected.

1919 Yet another disaster visited the state. This time it was a monster tornado that dipped down in Fergus Falls, destroying half the town. The toll was 59 killed, $3.5 million damage.

1920 Pipestone's thermometer read 74° on April 1, 8° the next day.

1921 Winds as high as 59 m.p.h. whipped up a snow blizzard in the north and a sand blizzard in the southwest on January 16. Tropical air invaded southern Minnesota on February 15, bringing thunderstorms and temperatures as high as 67° at Winona.

1922 Barometers rose and temperatures fell as a huge arctic high pressure settled over the state on January 21. The barometer at Collegeville read 31.11", a state record, and Itasca saw -51° on the 22nd. A real potpourri of weather came with a winter storm on February 21-23—thunderstorms preceded an ice storm, which was followed by a blizzard.

1923 The "Black Dust Blizzard" of February 12-14 left dark drifts of snow and North Dakota dirt across southwestern Minnesota. International Falls had its hottest day in history, 103°, on July 22.

1924 The mercury jumped 73°, from -32° to +41°, in only 24 hours at Pipestone on January 6.

1925 The moon's shadow made one of its rare sweeps of the earth on January 24, this time across northern Minnesota. Clear skies allowed views of the morning eclipse at International Falls, Cass Lake, Cusson and Marble, while clouds obscured the show at Duluth (although the *Herald* reported that chickens were "puzzled by the dark dawning" and stayed in their roosts).

An early heat wave sent the thermometer to 99° at Minneapolis and 100° at Tracy and New Ulm on May 22. Thirty-six hours later all three places stood at a freezing 32°. October was the coldest in 170 years of Twin Cities records and 95 years of statewide averages. With the averages more than 10° below normal, October was more like a typical November.

1927 A massive anticyclone set high-pressure records from Minnesota to North Carolina, including Duluth's barometer reading of 31.05".

1928 Lights were turned on the Twin Cities during daytime on February 19 as a cloud of dust swept in from the west.

1929 An early-season tornado on April 5 cut a 200-foot-wide path from Lake Minnetonka, across Minneapolis and Fridley, into Chisago County. Six people died.

1931 One of the nation's great trains, the "Empire Builder," was broadsided by a tornado near Moorhead on May 27. The train was knocked on its side, and one passenger was killed. On June 30, Canby soared to 110° after a toasty morning low of 87°. The 110° was a Minnesota June record, and the 87° was the hottest night any place in the state has ever enjoyed. A rare November tornado touched down near Maple Plain on the 16th. This year was the warmest of the 170 years, averaging 49.5° (6° above normal) at Minneapolis and 45.9° (4° above normal) statewide.

1933 Pigeon River Bridge, in the extreme northeastern tip of Minnesota, measured 28" of snow in 24 hours, the state's greatest one-day storm, on April 4-5. The summer of '33 was the warmest on record in Minneapolis, until 1988 came along. The first of the great duststorms that gave the "Dust Bowl" its name swept southwestern Minnesota on November 11-12, and blew dust east to New England. At the same time the same storm was fouling traffic in northwestern Minnesota with blizzard conditions.

1934 A series of spring duststorms began on April 13, and culminated with the great duststorm of May 9-10. Dust two miles deep rode gale-force winds behind a cold front, and low visibility grounded aircraft at Minneapolis Wold-Chamberlain field and halted car and

MINNESOTA HISTORICAL SOCIETY

A dust storm, circa 1938, turns two o'clock in the afternoon into semi-dusk in Minneapolis.

bus traffic in the Twin Cities. Gale-force winds downed trees and pushed gritty particles through closed windows. Drifting dust and sand blocked rural roads and filled drainage ditches. Lights were switched on in mid-afternoon in Fergus Falls as the dark cloud blotted out the sun. Hallock's temperature fell to 18° in the cold air behind the dusty front.

A heat wave began in earnest on May 16, and continued for the rest of the month. St. Paul soared to 107° on the 31st, setting an all-time record high for any month. Campbell, Fairmont, Faribault, New Ulm and Pipestone recorded 108°. It was Minnesota's hottest May ever, and marked an early start of one of the hottest and driest summers. The agricultural result was what has been termed "the worst crop year in history."

1935   More duststorms raged from late February into April. The summer was warmer than normal—but nowhere near as extreme as the summers of '34 and '36—and rainfall was near normal. There were 15 tornadoes in Minnesota during the year, a record not to be exceeded until 1957.

1936   This, more than any year in the nation's (and Minnesota's) history, was a year of weather extremes. Two states—both Dakotas—saw their coldest weather ever, 15 states (including both Dakotas) recorded their hottest days in history, and numerous places recorded their driest year. Statewide, February was Minnesota's second coldest month in 95 years with an average of -6.5°, while July's average of 76.2° was Minnesota's hottest month ever. The 169° spread between the state's extreme temperatures during the year was itself an extreme. January and February averaged 1.9° in Minneapolis, the coldest two-month period since 1875, and there were 36 consecutive nights with below zero temperatures. Warroad fell to 55° below on January 22, and Hallock averaged -14.4° in February. The cold lingered into April—on the 7th Minneapolis recorded 6° above.

Summer (especially July) was intensely hot. Hottest-ever readings came from Moorhead (114°), New Ulm (111°), Farmington and Fergus Falls (110°), Hallock and St. Peter (109°), Minneapolis and Rochester (108°), Bemidji, Detroit Lakes, Roseau, and St. Cloud (107°), Virginia (103°), and most other places in Minnesota. Even Duluth, the "Air-Conditioned City," recorded 106° in town and an amazing 108° at the harbor Coast Guard station. July's 81.4° average in Minneapolis made it the Twin Cities' hottest month in history, and Pipestone's average daily high temperature in July was 99.4°.

It was a dry year, too. Angus saw only 7.81" of precipitation all year, the lowest annual amount ever measured in the state. Averaged across the state, the annual precipitation of 18.08" was the third lowest on record.

1937   For the winter of 1936-37, Pigeon River Bridge recorded a total of 147.5" of precipitation, a Minnesota record. January was much colder than normal, but the rest of the year enjoyed normal temperatures and rainfall—a welcome relief from 1936! Two October snowstorms, on the 16th–17th and the 23rd, each dumped up to a foot of snow in northern Minnesota.

1938   Forest fires took 21 lives in northern Minnesota, October 9-10.

1939   After touching down in northern Hennepin County, a tornado leveled a three-block-wide path through Anoka, destroying more than 250 homes, killing nine residents, and injuring 222 more. The funnel divided the waters of the Mississippi River as it crossed, an event that has been compared to the biblical parting of the Red Sea.

1940   No doubt you've seen the famous film footage of the Tacoma Narrows Bridge, a.k.a. "Galloping Gertie," in Washington State swaying, twisting and finally collapsing, in gale-force winds. That was November 7, 1940. Four days later, after crossing the Rockies and re-intensifying over the central plains, the storm galloped across Minnesota as the legendary Armistice Day Storm. Over much of the state the onslaught began during the afternoon of the 11th, an unfortunate timing which—as in 1873 and 1888—trapped many outdoors. Among Minnesota's 49 fatalities were 20 duck hunters who froze as temperatures plunged from the 60s to below zero overnight. Minneapolis recorded 16.8" of snow, a storm record that stood until 1982, and Collegeville was buried under 26.6". The barometer in Duluth read 28.66", a reading normally reserved for hurricanes, and out on the Great Lakes the storm sent 59 sailors down with their ships.

1941   Beware the Ides of March... Four months after the Armistice Day Storm, another daytime blizzard struck on Saturday, March 15. Once again, many motorists were caught out on the road, and at least 32 people died in Minnesota, 39 more in North Dakota. Snow accumulations in the fast-moving storm were not impressive, but the high winds were—75 m.p.h. in Duluth and 85 m.p.h. in Grand Forks, North Dakota.

1942   A squall line crossed southern Minnesota at 70 m.p.h. on September 11, destroying 651 barns and killing five people in its 30-mile-wide, 180-mile-long path.

1944   January was the mildest in 98 years at Minneapolis and St. Paul, and the warmest on record for most of the state except for the southeast. Only 0.6" of snow fell at St. Paul, that following a snowless December.

1946   Snow flurries were reported at St. Paul's Holman Field on June 1. A tornado struck Wells and Mankato on August 17, killing 11.

1947   It was the hottest August in 170 years of record at Minneapolis–St. Paul. The thermometer at the airport reached or exceeded 100° four times. September 10 was a wet day at Hibbing, with 8.6" of rain descending in 24 hours.

1948   An airliner crashed during a thunderstorm near Winona on August 29, killing 37 people aboard.

1949   Minnesota's most powerful October windstorm ever blasted the state with winds gusting to 100 m.p.h. at Rochester and 89 m.p.h. at Minneapolis. Barometric pressure at International Falls fell to 28.70". Observers noted a hurricane-like calm as the storm center crossed the northwestern corner of the state, and dubbed the tempest a "land hurricane."

1950   Another "land hurricane" blasted Minnesota on May 5-6, whipping Duluth with winds measured at 88 m.p.h. Winds were clocked at 93 m.p.h. aboard a ship in Lake Superior. Duluth's—and Minnesota's—second greatest snowstorm in history socked the harbor city with 35.2", December 5-8, with 25.2" falling in 24 hours.

1951   Five people died as a tornado struck Richland (Hennepin County) and southwestern Minneapolis on July 20.

1952   Spring snow melt and river ice jams combined to produce one of the worst floods on record along the upper Mississippi and Red rivers. 11 lives lost, $198 million in damage.

1953   An ice storm coated wires 3" thick at Lake Benton, November 20-21.

1954   Snow covered most of Minnesota on May 2-3, with storm totals ranging from an inch in the south to 18" at Virginia. Clear weather on the morning of June 30 allowed many Minnesotans a perfect view of a total solar eclipse.

1955   Hail piled one foot deep at Rushmore, Houston County, on August 23.

1957   A tornado cut across Fargo and Moorhead on June 20, killing 10 and injuring 103 in its path.

1958   An enormous cyclone, centered in Minnesota, enveloped the entire United States on November 17-18. The circulation brought record warmth to the eastern states, record cold to the west, and 60 m.p.h. winds and 35 deaths to Minnesota.

1959   On May 12, a cold front packing winds to 84 m.p.h. at Hibbing and 74 m.p.h. at Duluth brought thick clouds of North Dakota dust, turning day to darkness and downing trees and power lines across northern Minnesota. Temperatures in the wake of the front fell as low as 22°.

1961   The remains of Hurricane Carla passed near Chicago on September 13, dumping torrential rains on Iowa, Wisconsin and Illinois. Extreme southeastern Minnesota received 1" to 2" of rain, but the heaviest rains just missed the state.

1962   A bitter March cold wave sent the mercury tumbling to -32° at Minneapolis–St. Paul Airport, -38° at International Falls, and -44° at Bemidji, all records for the month. Hail killed and maimed 130 great blue herons and great egrets at Shields Lake in Rice County on May 12.

1963   Four arctic outbreaks engulfed Minnesota in January. The most severe of these kept the temperature at Minneapolis–St. Paul below zero for 157 consecutive hours, from the 18th to the 23rd. In contrast to January's cold, this October was the warmest one in history across most of the state. Beardsley recorded 98° on the 5th, Minnesota's highest-ever October reading.

1964   One of the lowest low-pressure systems ever seen in Minnesota passed between St. Cloud and Minneapolis around noon on April 13. The barometer at Minneapolis–St. Paul dropped to 28.77" (a Twin Cities record) as the winds rose to 82 m.p.h. in gusts. West of the storm center up to 6" of snow fell. A November cold wave sent the mercury to -17° at Minneapolis–St. Paul on the 30th.

1965   Collegeville was buried by 66.4" of snow in March, the snowiest month ever measured in Minnesota. Duluth had a record 48" of snow covering the ground on March 18. The record snows in March led to record snow melt in April, which in turn led to record flooding along the upper Mississippi River. Along a 672-mile stretch of the Mississippi it was the highest flood in history, and at St. Paul the flood crest was 4 feet higher than any previous flood. Along some portions of the river the flooding went on for 43 days. The loss totaled 16 lives and $181 million damage.

On May 6, a swarm of 6 tornadoes touched down in between Sibley and Anoka counties. Fridley was ripped by two twisters 80 minutes apart; also hard-hit were Mounds View, Deephaven and Navarre. More than 900 homes, mobile homes, farm buildings, and businesses were destroyed, another 1,371 damaged, 16 people were killed and 683 injured. It was the worst disaster ever to befall the Twin Cities metropolitan area.

1966   The "Blizzard of '66" began on March 1 and lasted 4 days as the storm center wallowed in a looping track over South Dakota and southern Minnesota. Aitkin received 23" of snow, and after the blizzard was over International Falls had a record 37" lying on the ground. On the first day of spring, March 22, an "equinoctial storm" ushered in by a line of thunderstorms dumped 11" of snow on the Twin Cities in 12 hours. The wet snow was particularly effective at bringing down telephone lines.

For the second year in a row, heavy March snows produced severe April floods—this time in the Red River basin. The flooding was the worst since 1950, and in some places the worst ever.

On the 4th of July hailstones up to a foot in circumference (a state record) fell near Detroit Lakes. On October 14th an even larger hailstone, reportedly 16" in circumference, crashed through a truck windshield near Claremont in Dodge County. The same storm also brought a tornado near Albert Lea, winds to 80 m.p.h., lightning, and heavy rains that later changed to freezing rain and snow—all the seasons in a single storm!

1967   A quick blizzard on January 16 sent temperatures plummeting to record lows and caused the deaths of 7 Minnesotans in the severe cold, while shoveling snow, or in auto wrecks. Eight days later, on the 24th, a rare January lightning storm changed over to freezing rain. One inch of ice in the Twin Cities brought down power lines and tree limbs, leaving 10,000 homes without power.

Nine tornadoes struck southern Minnesota on April 30, killing 13 and injuring 65. Among the hard-hit towns were Albert Lea, Owatonna and Waseca. Tennis-ball size hail pummeled Willmar, and wind-whipped 15-foot waves on Lake Superior drowned three Duluth boys and a Coast Guard sailor who tried to rescue them. Meanwhile, northwestern Minnesota experienced near-blizzard conditions with light snow and high winds. In the wake of the storm, temperatures dipped to 6° at Crookston on May 3.

On June 30, thunderstorms with hail blown by 100-m.p.h. winds wiped out crops along a 40-mile-wide swath from Wheaton (Traverse County) to Stillwater. At Minneapolis–St. Paul the winds rolled mobile homes, downed TV towers, and left 200,000 home without electricity. A tornado swept through a cemetery near Roseau on July 25, but no injuries were reported.

1968   A small tornado damaged three farms near Truman, Martin County, on March 18—the earliest date a tornado had ever struck Minnesota. On June 13 a more significant tornado ravaged Tracy (Lyon County), killing 9 people, destroying 111 homes, and damaging more than 200 other buildings. These were but two of the 34 tornadoes reported in Minnesota during 1968, an all-time record.

1969   Six blizzards and several snow and ice storms during December (1968) and January accumulated 30" to 50" deep across much of northern Minnesota. Wildlife—particularly pheasants and deer—suffered tremendously from the deep snow, and by reducing the amount of sunlight reaching into shallow lakes, the snow reduced the oxygen production in the water, leading to widespread fish kills. When the spring snowmelt arrived in April, nearly all major rivers in the state (particularly the Red River of the North and the Mississippi) flooded. Nine people drowned and damage totaled $150 million. On August 6 a widespread tornado outbreak raked the north woods. It started with a waterspout on Lake Bemidji and, over the course of the afternoon, 12 tornadoes left 15 dead and 106 injured in Cass, Aitkin, Itasca and St. Louis counties. Most of the deaths occurred as a behemoth 1.5-mile-wide twister roared through the town of Outing.

1970   Record early-season snow amounts of 10" to 14" fell across northwestern Minnesota on October 8-10. On the afternoon of December 3 a snowburst, punctuated by thunder and lightning, dumped a foot of snow from Grand Rapids to Duluth.

1971   One of the strongest low-pressure system's in Minnesota's history crossed the state on February 26-27. The barometer fell to 28.77" at Minneapolis–St. Paul and 28.75" at Duluth. North and west of the low, freezing rain combined with 10"-18" of snow brought down power lines, leaving areas around Virginia in the dark for five days.

Slow-moving, concentrated thunderstorms dumped up to 10" of rain in a 6-by-12-mile area near Bird Island. In Birch Coulee State Park, flood water 20 feet deep washed away roads, picnic tables and outhouses.

Widespread hail rattled a 100-mile-wide swath cutting from the northwest to southeast corners of the state on July 14. There were more than 2,000 individual hail damage reports. Along the shores of Lake Alexander in Morrison County, a brush fire spawned a 10-foot-wide, 50-foot-high "fire whirl" that moved out onto the lake, overturned a 1,800-pound pontoon boat, and dissipated as it came back ashore. This occurred on September 18.

1972   The temperature fell to 53° below near International Falls on January 15. On January 24 a blizzard swept southwestern Minnesota with 4" to 10" snows whipped by winds as high as 72 m.p.h. at Worthington. Schools closed at noon, but many buses became stranded in the snow, forcing the children to stay at farm houses.

A cold and wet spring (particularly May) delayed crop planting by several weeks. On May 1 strong northeast winds piled ice 25 feet deep along the southern shore of Mille Lacs Lake, closing Highway 169. On Lake Superior icebergs were spotted off Duluth on June 9.

On the night of July 21-22 incessant thunderstorms in a 25-mile-wide, 150-mile-long band stretching east-west across the center of the state dumped 4" to 14" of rain. With the exception of Interstate 25, every highway in this band was impassable for up to 2 weeks, and flood damage totaled $20 million. The 14" rainfall at the Jaschki farm, near Little Falls in Morrison County, is Minnesota's record one-day total. Back-to-back flash floods, 80 hours apart, struck Duluth on August 16 and 20, with yet another flood on September 20. On October 17 an early snow in southern Minnesota ended a rather short crop growing season. A New Year's Eve blizzard ended Minnesota's coldest year since 1971 with a statewide average temperature of 38°.

1973   Early navigational opening on Lake Superior—the opposite of 1972! Ball lightning, mysterious glowing blobs ever so rarely observed during thunderstorms, was seen inside a house near St. Cloud on June 8, "dancing around...leaving bullet-sized holes in walls and larger holes in ceilings," according to the National Weather Service report. A 15-minute hailstorm northeast of Grand Rapids on June 22 piled hail 7" deep, stopping traffic on Highway 169.

1974   On May 28, golf ball to baseball sized hail piled waist deep near Amboy, south of Mankato, shredding 80 percent of the corn crop. Six days later pea-size hail piled 1' to 3' deep at Cokato in Wright County.

On June 20, "Dark Thursday," a 10-mile-high mass of thunderstorms brought darkness at noon to the Twin Cities area. Street lights turned on and birds went to bed as brightness levels (measured at the University of Minnesota weather station in St. Paul) dimmed to less than 1 percent of the normal noontime amount. High winds also brought down an enormous number of trees and branches. A widespread frost and freeze on September 3—the earliest on record in many places—put a sudden end to the growing season. Losses to corn, soybean, and honey production exceeded $100 million.

1975   It was a stormy year... Rated by the National Weather Service as Minnesota's "Storm of the Century," a severe blizzard blasted the entire state with 1 to 2 feet of snow, winds as high as 80 m.p.h., and below-zero temperatures. Drifts reaching 20 feet in height closed virtually every road in the state—some for as long as 11 days—to all traffic except snowmobiles. The storm center tracked from south to north across the state, sending the barometer to record lows at Rochester (28.63"), Minneapolis–St. Paul (28.62"), and Duluth (28.55", a state record). A train with 168 aboard was trapped near Willmar, 6,000 homes lost power in western Minnesota, 15,000 head of livestock froze, and the Red Cross sheltered 16,672 people. The snow and cold claimed 14 lives, and 21 more died of heart attacks while digging out.

Two early spring blizzards swept Minnesota on March 23-24 and 26-29. Hardest hit was Duluth, which received a foot of snow from each storm, and where 100-m.p.h. winds and 20-foot waves during the first storm devastated lake front businesses and beaches.

On June 28-29 torrential downpours totaling 14" at Ulen (northeast of Moorhead) and more than 18 in nearby North Dakota unleashed devastating floods along the Red River. Along with the rains, two massive tornadoes, three fourths and one mile wide, churned up farmland near Moorhead, damaging several buildings but injuring no one. Two days later and 100 miles farther north another storm dumped up to 10" of rain. At the peak of the flood nearly 4,000 square miles were under water, and losses to crops, roads and bridges reached $273 million.

Minnesota's second-strongest earthquake since 1860, a 5 on the Richter scale, cracked foundations and sidewalks in Stevens County on July 9.

The 730-foot ore carrier, the *Edmund Fitzgerald,* went down in high seas and hurricane-force winds over eastern Lake Superior on November 10, a day after leaving Superior harbor.

1976   On the morning of January 10, icy roads and poor visibility during a 3" snow-fall resulted in dozens of chain-reaction car wrecks in the Twin Cities area. About 1,200 vehicles were involved in accidents, including 42 in a single pile-up in Fridley. There were no deaths. Statewide, 1976 was the second driest year for the period of record, 1895-1990, with an average precipitation of only 15.75". July and August were particularly hot and dry, and the driest May on record—0.83" statewide—helped kindle 300,000 acres of brush and forest fires.

1977   Minnesota's wettest year on record. The statewide average of 33.92" was twice that of 1976. This moisture flip-flop was a deja vu of 1910-1911, when the state's driest year was followed by one of the wettest. At Minneapolis–St. Paul it was the coldest January since 1912, and at 5 a.m. January 28 the wind chill factor read 78° below. On August 26 a tornado skipped along an 85-mile-long path from Fergus Falls to Brainerd, injuring 23. On September 8 a farm near Palisade, Aitkin County, was struck by a tornado for the second time in two years.

1978   An early morning tornado cut a 75-mile-long path across northwestern Minnesota on July 5, leveling one third of the town of Gary, destroying dozens of buildings and mobile homes in Fosston and Clearbrook, and killing 4. That evening a different storm dropped 5.8" of rain on Rochester, a record, causing the worst flooding in the city's history. Water 6' or more deep inundated one fourth of Rochester, sweeping away cars, trees, and bridges. Three patients and a nurse's aide drowned in a stalled elevator at a nursing home.

1979   A line of violent thunderstorms swept across the southern half of Minnesota on the evening of June 19, uprooting trees, downing power lines, flattening crops, and injuring 25 people.

1980   It was Minnesota's driest April since 1927, with a statewide average precipitation of a mere 0.51". The lack of rain, combined with warm and windy days with low humidity, set the stage for widespread brush and forest fires that consumed more than 80,000 acres. While most were in the central and east-central counties. Most of the fires were ignited by burning trash, some started from sparks off the wheels of passing trains, and one was started by someone trying to brand his horse!

On July 15 a thunderstorm plowed through the southern suburbs of metropolitan Minneapolis–St. Paul with straight-line winds up to 110 m.p.h. Damage to homes and apartments totaled $43 million, and power was knocked out to 100,000 homes. Three weeks later, on August 6, a severe thunderstorm from North Dakota roared down Interstate 94 to Minneapolis–St. Paul with winds clocked at 90 m.p.h. This time 118,500 homes were without power. On September 19 hail as large as baseballs in St. Paul smashed numerous car windshields and damaged 75 to 95 percent of the glass in that city's greenhouses.

1981   A tornado on June 14 tracked from Edina to Roseville by way of downtown Minneapolis, injuring 83 and killing 1 in its 2½-block-wide path. During a thunderstorm in Clearwater County on August 5, ball lightning reportedly entered a house through the telephone and rolled across a piano keyboard and around the living room. Damage was minor.

Ten inches of wet, heavy snow on November 18-19 overloaded the inflatable fabric dome of the Hubert Humphrey Metrodome in Minneapolis, causing it to collapse, tear and deflate.

1982   January provided two weather double whammies. Wind chill indices on the 9th exceeded 100° below zero in northern Minnesota, and on the 17th—"Cold Sunday"— actual temperatures fell to 52° below at Tower and Embarrass. Then Minneapolis was hit by two record-setting snowstorms, just two days apart! 17.1" on the 20th and 19.9" on the 22nd–23rd set new 24-hour and single-storm records, respectively. (Records are made to be broken, though, so look at 1991, below.) Other Twin Cities records: 38" snow depth on the ground, and 44" total snowfall for the month.

Up to an inch of ice accumulated in southeastern Minnesota on December 27-28, downing tree limbs and power lines. North of the band of ice, Minneapolis–St. Paul received 16.5" of snow.

1983   While most of the U.S. suffered stormy onslaughts induced by "el niño" (a massive warming of the tropical Pacific Ocean), Minnesota basked in winter temperatures averaging 6° to 8° above normal. St. Paul's low for the entire 1982-83 winter was only -9°, the highest winter low ever. The honeymoon didn't last forever, though... the final month of the year was the coldest December on record across the state. Most of the state remained below zero from December 16 through Christmas. On July 3, straight-line thunderstorm winds estimated in the 100-150 m.p.h. range swept a narrow, 2- to 6-mile-wide strip from Maple Grove (Hennepin County) to near Taylors Falls (Chisago County) and into Wisconsin, ripping roofs from homes and shopping malls. A powerful tornado embedded in the storm struck Andover (Anoka County). On the 19th thunderstorms raked an area from Alexandria (where the wind gauge was pegged at 117+ m.p.h.) to the Twin Cities, causing power outages to 250,000 customers.

1984   A cold front bringing 1" to 2" of snow whipped by 80 m.p.h. gusts, described as a "wall of white," roared southeast across Minnesota on the afternoon of February 4. The sudden onslaught stranded hundreds in cars and fish houses, or simply outdoors, and 16 died. Among the dead were a family of six stuck in their car near Windom.

The biggest snowstorm ever so late in the season dropped 9.7" on Minneapolis–St. Paul on April 29-30, and pushed the season's total to 98.4", making it the snowiest winter ever.

1985   A blizzard on March 3-4 buried the entire state under 6" to 24" of snow. Hardest hit was Duluth, where winds measuring over 90 m.p.h. along the harbor whipped 15" of snow into mountainous drifts. The schools at International Falls closed for their first "snow day" in history. On July 3 a tornado became a waterspout when it went across Mille Lacs Lake, and regained tornado status when it came ashore again. A brisk November cold wave sent the mercury tumbling to 32° below zero on the 28th at International Falls.

1986   Thunderstorm winds reaching 85 m.p.h. at Duluth Harbor blew three ore carriers across St. Louis Bay. Several small tornadoes touched down nearby. On July 18 "the world's most photographed tornado" (possibly) was seen live on the 5 o'clock news as a television helicopter caught it churning up trees at the Springbrook Nature Center (north of Minneapolis).

MINNESOTA'S GREATEST BLIZZARD

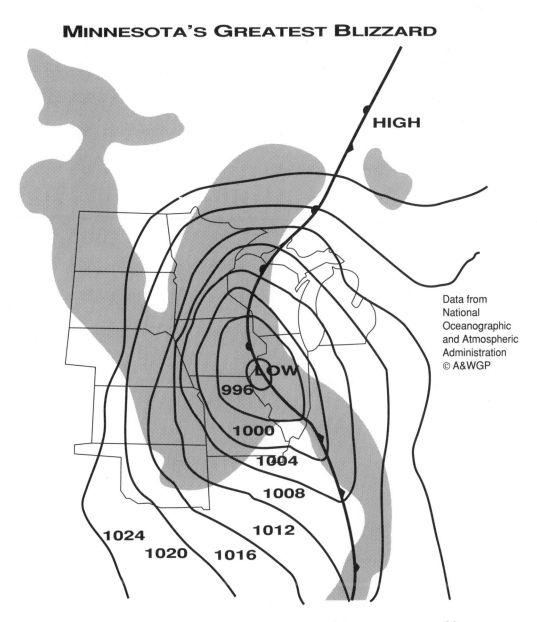

HIGH

Data from
National
Oceanographic
and Atmospheric
Administration
© A&WGP

LOW

996

1000

1004

1008

1024   1012

1020   1016

The weather map at 6 a.m. on November 1, 1991, at the height of the greatest storm in Minnesota history. The low pressure is centered on the Iowa–Illinois border (the previous day at this same time it was near Houston and the following day at Thunder Bay, Ontario). North of the low center a westward-moving warm front becomes a stationary front as it extends into Canada. An eastward-moving cold front extends south from the low across Illinois. The curving contour lines (or "isobars") around the low give pressure in "millibars," a metric unit used by meteorologists. At the center of the low, the 996 millibar pressure equals 29.41" of mercury. At the edge of the storm the 1024 millibars equals 30.24". The shaded area covers regions experiencing rain or snow at 6 a.m. All data in the map are based on information from surface observers.

1987 Winds gusting to 59 m.p.h. on February 2 sent 40 to 50 ice houses skidding across Lake Washington in Le Sueur County. A tornado that damaged more than 300 homes in Maple Grove marked the start of the July 23-24 "Superstorm." The storm ended with a record 10.00" of rain falling in 6.5 hours on Minneapolis–St. Paul Airport. The rains fell on ground saturated by another downpour on the 20th, and cumulative totals reached 12" to 14" in some places. Flood waters damaged 9,000 homes and businesses. Two people died in the floods, including one who drove around a police barricade into a flooded creek. Statewide, the year's average temperature of 45.7° was the second warmest in the past century.

1988 The "Year of the Drought" brought a hot, dry summer that stunted crops across the upper Midwest. Overall crop production was 40 percent less than the 1984-1987 average. The state maximum of 110° at Montevideo was the highest since the Dust Bowl years; Minneapolis and St. Paul each recorded 105°. It was also the Twin Cities' longest and hottest summer in history, with the May through August average temperature exceeding the 1936 record by 2°. St. Paul saw 47 days reach 90° or hotter, another record.

1989 Twenty-four to 26" of snow buried the Fargo-Moorhead area under its biggest snowstorm ever, January 6-8. After the snow stopped, a cold front brought 50 m.p.h. winds and ground blizzards that shut down the Red River Valley. Rains and melting snow in late March gave the valley its worst flooding since 1969.

On May 24, 9 tornadoes and numerous funnel clouds were spotted in southern Minnesota. There were no injuries and damage was relatively moderate, but winds were clocked at 109 m.p.h. at the Albert Lea airport as a twister touched down. A pre-Christmas cold wave kept the mercury at Minneapolis–St. Paul below zero for 116 consecutive hours.

1990 January was Minnesota's second-warmest in the past 95 years, and came on the heels of the sixth-coldest December. Lightning struck and exploded a pine tree in Olmsted County on August 25, sending pieces flying up to 500 feet away. The lightning then jumped to a TV antenna on a nearby house, blowing out windows and removing the garage door. Nine inches of rain in the Duluth area washed out a million dollars worth of roads on September 5-6.

1991 Early spring heat sent the mercury to 81° at International Falls and above 90° across southeastern Minnesota on April 6. Lightning killed a spectator at the U.S. Open golf tournament in Chaska on June 13. Duluth was dusted by 2.5" of snow on September 18, five days before the end of summer, the harbor city's largest and earliest September snow ever.

A massive snowstorm tracked from south to north across Minnesota on Halloween night and the next day, burying the Twin Cities under 26" of snow. Roseville received 30", and Duluth nearly disappeared under 36.9" of fluffy powder. The storm totals were the greatest ever measured in all three places, while Duluth's total was the deepest snowfall in Minnesota history. November's snowfall total of 46.9" made it Minneapolis–St. Paul's snowiest month ever, and -3° on November 2 was the Twin Cities' earliest below zero temperature reading.

RESOURCES

■■■■■■■■■■■■■■■■■■■■■■■■■■■■■

In a way, *Minnesota Weather* is like a medium pizza—enough to satisfy some folks' interest in the weather, but a mere appetizer for many others. If you're still hungry, here are some suggestions about where to go next.

BOOKS

Weather, by Lehr, Burnett, and Zim, Golden Press, New York. The first edition of this little volume appeared in 1957 and the contents have been updated several times since. It's compact but comprehensive, easy to read and well illustrated, and I have recommended it to audiences from Cub Scouts to mountain climbers. It was my first weather book, oh so many years ago! A beautiful book about Minnesota's weather in general is *Prairie Skies,* by Paul Douglas (Voyageur Press, P.O. Box 338, Stillwater, MN 55082).

Unfortunately, this one's out of print, but the *WCCO Weather Almanac 1975,* by Bruce Watson (Freshwater Biological Research Foundation, P.O. Box 90, Navarre, MN 55392) should be in your library. It's absolutely chock full of weather facts and figures. A mere fraction of these facts and figures appear in the annual *Minnesota Weatherguide Calendar,* written by Bruce Watson and James Gilbert and published by the Freshwater Foundation, WCCO-TV (90 South 11th St., Minneapolis, MN 55403), and the Science Museum of Minnesota.

Minnesotans are particularly fond of books about specific weather events. The list of these books reads like a 1970s disaster film festival:

All Hell Broke Loose, written and published by William Hull, 6833 Creston Road, Edina, MN 55435, compiles 167 personal accounts of the 1940 Armistice Day blizzard.

From the Ashes, by Grace Swenson (Croixside Press, Stillwater, MN) and *Wall of Flames,* by Lawrence Larsen (North Dakota Institute for Regional Studies, Fargo, ND), are about the Hinckley fire of 1894. Also see *The Fires of Autumn: The Cloquet–Moose Lake Fires of 1918,* by Francis Carroll and Franklin Raiter (Minnesota Historical Society Press, St. Paul, MN 55101).

Then there's *The Great Fergus Falls Cyclone of June 22, 1918,* by Lance Johnson (Victor Lundeen Co., Fergus Falls, MN 56537), whose title is self-explanatory.

Anyone intrigued by maritime weather at its worst should read *Shipwrecks of Lake Superior,* edited by James Marshall and published by Lake Superior Magazine, P.O. Box 16417, Duluth, MN 55816-6417, or *Lake Superior Shipwrecks,* by Julius Wolff, Jr., available from the Lake Superior Marine Museum Association, P.O. Box 177, Duluth, MN 55801-0177.

Superbly detailed books about weather history and events in Minnesota and the rest of the United States are David M. Ludlum's series on *Early American Winters* (volumes I and II) and *Early American Tornadoes,* along with his *The American Weather Book.* All are available from the American Meteorological Society, 45 Beacon Street, Boston, MA 02108.

The A.M.S. also sells the *International Cloud Atlas,* Volume II, a must for serious cloud watchers. Published in 1987 by the World Meteorological Organization, this lavish (and expensive—$85) volume contains more than 200 photographs of clouds and other weather phenomena and is the international standard for identifying cloud types. Much more affordable are the cloud charts (and assorted teaching aids) from How the Weatherworks, 1522 Baylor Avenue, Rockville, MD 20850, and For Spacious Skies, 54 Webb Street, Lexington, MA 02173. Between these extremes, for $18 you can get *The Audubon Society Field Guide to North American Weather* (Alfred Knopf, New York, 1991), which has a spectacular selection of photographs.

If you're curious about the weather of other parts of the U.S., I can't resist recommending *Skywatch: The Western Weather Guide* and *Skywatch: The Eastern Weather Guide,* by Richard A. Keen, published by Fulcrum, 350 Indiana Street, Suite 350, Golden, CO 80401.

PERIODICALS

Weatherwise, published six times a year by Heldref Publications, 4000 Albemarle Street N.W., Washington, D.C. 20016. For more than 40 years this has been the only magazine in America devoted solely to weather. Its articles cover weather research, history, and recent weather events.

Science News reports on the latest discoveries in all the sciences, including meteorology. It's published weekly by Science Service, 231 West Center Street, Marion, OH 43305.

American Weather Observer is a monthly tabloid that lists weather reports from amateur weather watchers around the country, including your own, if you wish. Write to the Association of American Weather Observers, P.O. Box 455, 401 Whitney Blvd., Belvidere, IL 61008.

A must for heavy weather addicts is *Storm Track,* a bi-monthly newsletter for storm chasers and watchers published by Tim Marshall, 1336 Brazos Blvd., Lewisville, TX 75067, for $10 a year. It's informal and enthusiastic, and features a cartoon called "Funnel Funny"!

The National Weather Association, 4400 Stamp Road, Room 404, Temple Hills, MD 20748, publishes the *National Weather Digest* along with slide sets and a manual for interpreting weather satellite pictures. Articles in the *Digest* are written by real live weather forecasters about specific weather events, and lend an appreciation for what these people do for a living.

The *Bulletin of the American Meteorological Society* is directed to the professional meteorologist, but amateurs will enjoy many of the articles and news notes. It's free to A.M.S. members but quite expensive otherwise (that's what libraries are for). The Society's address is: 45 Beacon St., Boston, MA 02108.

Four times a year *Mariners Weather Log* comes out with articles on ocean and Great Lakes weather. There's even practical advice like how to dodge waterspouts approaching your boat! It's $6 a year from the Superintendent of Documents (see U.S. Government Publications, below), and you can get a free sample copy from National Oceanographic Data Center, NOAA/NESDIS E/OC21, Universal Building, Room 412, Washington, DC 20235.

UNIVERSITY OF MINNESOTA PUBLICATIONS

The University of Minnesota has a selection of publications on the climate of Minnesota. Topics range from drought and floods to wind power and snowfall, and prices are extremely reasonable. Write to the University of Minnesota, Minnesota Extension Service, Distribution Center, 3 Coffey Hall, 1420 Eckles Ave., St. Paul, MN 55108-1030.

U.S. GOVERNMENT PUBLICATIONS

The federal government also publishes a variety of reasonably-priced climate- and weather-related publications. The Superintendent of Documents, U.S. Government Printing Office, Washington, D.C. 20402 has a general catalog, a special catalog of weather-related publications (ask for "Subject Bibliography #234—Weather"), and a monthly listing of new books.

The National Climatic Data Center, Federal Building, Asheville, NC 28801-2696 publishes tons of climate data for all sorts of locations. Write for their free list of "Selected Climatological Publications." Among these are:

Storm Data describes hundreds of storms, from hurricanes to dust devils, that strike the U.S.A. each month. There are maps, photos, and statistics—a bonanza for storm lovers!

Local Climatological Data—Monthly summaries of daily and hourly weather, available for five cities in Minnesota: Minneapolis–St. Paul, International Falls, Duluth, Rochester, and St. Cloud.

Climatological Data, Minnesota—Monthly summaries of temperature, rainfall, snow and other weather data at dozens of cities and towns from Hallock to Winona.

Climates of the States: Minnesota. Published for each state of the Union, these informative booklets describe the state's climate in words, numbers and maps. They include several pages of tabulated statistics about temperature, wind, snow, and the like for selected cities.

The Department of Agriculture, in cooperation with NOAA, puts out a *Weekly Weather and Crop Bulletin* that reports on weather conditions across the nation and around the world, with emphasis on agricultural impacts. It has been published weekly since 1872. Write NOAA/USDA, Joint Agricultural Weather Facility, USDA South Building, Room 5844, Washington, DC 20250.

AUDIOVISUALS

Films, videos, and slide sets about various aspects of the weather abound, if you know where to look. Edward A. Brotak, Atmospheric Sciences Program, UNC Asheville, NC 28804 has put together a long list of audiovisuals that you can buy or rent. The list costs two dollars.

The National Weather Service has a wide selection of pamphlets, slide sets and films available to schools, groups and individuals for purchase or loan. Their catalog of Weather and Flood Hazard Awareness Material can be obtained from: National Weather Service, Disaster Preparedness Staff W/OM11x1, Silver Spring Metro Center II, East-West Highway, Silver Spring, MD 20910, or from your local NWS office.

The Aurora Color Television Project, Geophysical Institute, University of Alaska, Fairbanks, AK 99775-0800, has a wonderful 24-minute video of the aurora borealis at its best (set to classical music!) It costs about $1.50 a minute, but if you like the northern lights, it's worth it.

DAILY WEATHER INFORMATION

Weather will never really make much sense unless you follow it each and every day. You don't have to take your own records; there's plenty of data available in the media and elsewhere. Along with the daily high and low temperatures across the country, most newspapers carry weather maps, satellite photos, and lists of daily high and low temperatures. However, newspaper maps aren't very informative. For a good, detailed weather map, I recommend the daily surface and upper-air maps published in weekly booklets by the Climate Analysis Center, Room 808, World Weather Building, Washington, D.C. 20233. They're $60 a year.

Television weather broadcasts vary in quality; some of the better ones can actually be learning experiences. Minnesota has been blessed with some of the most informative weathercasts and most informed weathercasters in the business. Most show time-lapse satellite photographs of moving storms and clouds. These space views of the weather give a perspective on the workings of the weather that was unavailable just 20 years ago. Watch them for a while and you'll get a real feel for how storms grow, move and die. Probably the most complete broadcast television weather report is "A.M. Weather." Produced in cooperation with the National Weather Service, this 15-minute report airs weekday mornings on most public television stations. Write to A.M. Weather, Owings Mill, MD 21117 for a brochure and station listing.

On cable television, "The Weather Channel" gives comprehensive, continuous and current weather reports. There's also a local weather channel (operated by WCCO-TV, Minneapolis), and Minnesota Public Television has continuous aviation weather on yet another channel. That makes Minnesota the only place in the country where you can tune in three different weather channels!

WEATHER ON THE RADIO

The weather is a subject of passing fancy to some and passionate interest to others. However, for many people—notably mariners, aviators and truckers—the whims of the winds are matters of economic welfare and even personal safety. To fill the needs of these people, an amazing variety of weather information is broadcast over a variety of radio frequencies. The airwaves are free, and you're all welcome to listen to these broadcasts—all you need is the proper radio for the frequency band of the broadcast. Here's a sampler of what's available:

AM Radio. Of course, you can hear your local weather forecast on an ordinary AM Radio. At night, when the electrons in the high atmosphere settle down and form a sort of a mirror to radio waves, you can pick up AM stations hundreds of miles away. It's fun to listen to what the weather is like in remote places such as St. Louis (1120 kilohertz, or "kHz"), Denver (850 kHz) and Winnipeg (580 kHz), and the information can be useful in making your own local forecasts. I recall some dramatic live descriptions of the eye of Hurricane Betsy when it passed over New Orleans (870 kHz) in 1965. Some stations, like Fort Worth (820 kHz), broadcast detailed national "Weather Along the Highways" reports to motorists and truckers.

Weather Radio. For up-to-date local weather information, your best bet by far is your nearest National Weather Service "Weather Radio" station. The continuous broadcasts give forecasts, warnings and observations for the area covered by the 25- to 50-mile range of the stations. There are hundreds of these stations in the U.S.A. and dozens in Canada; Minnesotans can listen to broadcasts from Detroit Lakes, Duluth, International Falls, Mankato, Minneapolis, Rochester, St. Cloud, Thief River Falls, Willmar, Fargo (ND), Sioux Falls (SD), La Crosse (WI), and Thunder Bay (Ontario). The National Weather Service, Attn: W/OM15x2, NOAA, Silver Spring, MD 20910 has a free brochure and station list describing the service. You can listen to these weather broadcasts on "police band" radios and scanners, as well as on special Weather Radios designed solely for these broadcasts. Some weather radios sound an alarm or switch on automatically whenever the local station broadcasts a severe weather warning! Several models in the $20 to $50 range are available from Maxon (8610 NW 107th Terrace, Kansas City, MO 64153; these are sold in electronics, hardware and department stores) and from Radio Shack.

Aviation and Marine Radio. Those who live near airports or seaports (and Great Lake ports) will find more sources of weather information in the "Very High Frequency" (VHF) marine (156-162 MHz) and aviation (108-136 MHz) bands. Some broadcast continuous weather reports, while others send out warnings and answer requests for specific information. One particularly interesting aviation frequency is 122 MHz, where pilots report their airborne weather observations to the ground. You can buy special marine and aviation radios to receive these transmissions, or listen on the VHF bands of multi-band radios and scanners (make sure the radio includes the aviation band). Excellent guides to marine weather broadcasts are the "Marine Weather Services Charts" that show, in map format, weather broadcast stations for Lake Superior and 14 other coastal regions of the United States, in-

131

cluding Alaska, Hawaii and Puerto Rico. They're $1.25 each from the National Ocean Service, Distribution Branch N/CG33, Riverdale MD 20737-1199, or from marine supply shops. Canadian broadcast schedules appear in "Radio Aids to Marine Navigation," available from the Canadian Government Publishing Center, Ottawa, Ontario K1A 0S9.

Ham Radio. When severe weather threatens, the National Weather Service relies on volunteer spotters to call in sightings of hail, funnel clouds, and such. Many of these spotters are amateur radio operators (or "hams") out in their cars with their mobile radio rigs. If you want to listen to these live reports, tune your radio or scanner to the 144-148 MHz band; if you would rather be out there yourself watching and reporting the weather, ask your local Weather Service or Civil Defense office about joining the "Skywarn" program.

Shortwave Radio. To hear some truly exotic weather reports, get a shortwave radio. The so-called shortwave band, 2 to 30 MHz (or 2,000 to 30,000 kHz), is unique in the radio spectrum in that its signals can travel literally around the world. They do this by reflecting off ionospheric layers, like AM radio waves, but since the higher frequencies of shortwave signals bounce off higher layers of the ionosphere, they travel farther. I've been able to pick up weather reports from Africa, Australia and Siberia! As you toast your toes by the fireplace on a subzero night, you can listen to hurricane advisories from Fiji. Some frequencies of interest to Minnesotans are:

2514, 4369, 4381, and 8794 kHz—Station WLC in Rogers City, Michigan, broadcasts Great Lakes weather forecasts and warnings, along with shipboard weather reports, several times a day. Schedules are subject to change, but try 3:45 a.m., 9:45 a.m., 3:45 p.m., and 9:45 p.m. Central Time.

3485, 6604, 10051, and 13270 kHz—Continuous airport weather reports from the eastern parts of the U.S. and Canada, transmitted from New York and Gander, Newfoundland. At approximately 5 and 35 minutes past each hour you'll hear the latest weather report from Minneapolis–St. Paul International Airport. These broadcasts are aimed at transatlantic airliners and can usually be heard in Europe, so next time you're visiting Finland you can listen to the weather back home!

6753 and 15035 kHz—Canadian and Arctic weather reports broadcast from Edmonton, Alberta; Trenton, Ontario; and St. John's, Newfoundland, at 20, 30 and 40 minutes (respectively) past each hour. When Edmonton reports temperatures below -30° (remember, Canadians use Celsius degrees), watch out—a cold wave may be on its way.

10090 and 13279 kHz—Siberian weather reports are broadcast from Khabarovsk from 5 to 10 and 35 to 40 minutes past each hour. The signal is faint and it's a tough station to catch, but worth it if you want to hear about a place that's colder than Minnesota!

6673, 8893, 10015, 11246, 13244, 13267, and 13354 kHz—Just some of the frequencies used by Air Force and NOAA "Hurricane Hunter" flights. You might even hear a report from the eye of a hurricane!

3860 kHz—Every day at 6:15 p.m. members of the Minnesota Amateur Weather Net (hams who have weather stations) get together on the air to trade weather reports from all across the state. South Dakotans gather for the same purpose on 3960 kHz at 8:00 a.m.

2500, 5000, 10000, 15000, and 20000 kHz—Station WWV in Fort Collins, CO, the nation's official time station, broadcasts beeps every second (exactly!) 24 hours a day, along with storm warnings for the Atlantic, Caribbean, Gulf of Mexico, and North Pacific beginning at 8 minutes past each hour. On good days you might hear storm warnings for the South Pacific from WWVH (Hawaii), on the same frequencies, at 48 minutes past the hour. WWV also broadcasts solar activity reports at 18 minutes past the hour. If the report predicts a "major" or "severe" geomagnetic storm, keep your eyes on the sky—there may be some northern lights. You can hear the same solar report by dialing 303-497-3235.

Most general stores don't carry shortwave radios, so you'll have to shop around. Perhaps the best one that is readily available is the Radio Shack DX-440 (I've got one). For a wider selection, check the specialty shops like Electronic Equipment Bank (137 Church St. N.W., Vienna, VA 22180), Universal Radio (1280 Aida Drive, Reynoldsburg, OH 43068), or Grove Enterprises (P.O. Box 98, Brasstown, NC 28902), or peruse the ads in one of the monthly radio magazines, like *Monitoring Times* (same address as Grove Enterprises) or *Popular Communications* (76 North Broadway, Hicksville, NY 11801).

A suitable radio will cost at least $150; if you want to spend less, try your luck at a local Amateur Radio Club swap meet (or "Hamfest"). The motto of these swap meets is "caveat emptor," so be sure the thing works before you walk out with it! Except for the time signal station WWV, all of these weather broadcasts are in Single Side Band (SSB) mode, so get a radio with a SSB switch or a Beat Frequency Oscillator (BFO) dial. Also make sure the radio can tune in the frequency bands you want. Finally, don't forget the antenna—for less than $10, you can string up a 50-foot wire that will work wonders.

Weather Fax. With a good shortwave radio, a computer, and a "demodulator" connecting the two, you can receive facsimile weather maps broadcast by the U.S. Air Force and the U.S. and Canadian Coast Guards. Starting from scratch, the entire setup could cost $1,000 or more, but it's a lot less if the computer is already on your desk. The least expensive demodulator I know of is made by Software Systems Consulting, 615 S. El Camino Real, San Clemente, CA 92672. You can also subscribe to over-the-wire fax services; check the ads in the *Bulletin of the American Meteorological Society* or *Weatherwise*.

Weather Satellites. You can skip the middleman and get satellite photos straight from the source by tuning in the satellites as they pass overhead. All you need is a good radio tuned to the proper VHF or UHF (Ultra-High Frequency) frequencies, a computer, and the appropriate software. For some satellites you don't even need a special antenna. Once more, look in the radio magazines for details.

A note about frequencies. The broadcast frequencies listed above are in kilohertz (KHz) and megahertz (MHz), formerly known as kilocycles and megacycles. One megahertz equals 1,000 kilohertz, so, for example, the standard AM broadcast band extends from 530 to 1600 kHz, or 0.53 to 1.6 MHz. Generally, frequencies less than 10,000 kHz (10 MHz) are received better at night, and higher frequencies are stronger during the day.

Thunder and Lightning. Yes, the weather itself broadcasts on a wide range of radio frequencies. You have doubtlessly heard the annoying static from nearby thunderstorms on your AM radio—that's because your cheap little radio is actually a pretty good lightning detector. Just tune the radio between stations, and you'll hear every lightning strike within 50 miles (farther at night). After a bit of practice, you'll be able to gauge the distance and intensity of the storm by noting how loud and frequent the static crashes are. If your radio has a signal strength meter, or "Vu-meter," the meter reading of the static will go up as the storm gets closer. Another trick is to rotate the radio until the static level drops off or disappears. At that point, the antenna (usually a black rod with copper wire coiled around it, running lengthwise inside the case) points directly at the storm. You may have to guess which end of the antenna is pointed toward the storm, though. Years ago the Forest Service used direction-finding radios to locate lightning storms for fire fighting purposes. Now, you can use your radio to wisely decide when to shut off your computer or get out of (or off of) the water.

WEATHER ON YOUR COMPUTER

Your computer is also interested in the weather. Humor it, or it may get back at you. Fortunately, a rapidly growing number of weather-related products and services can turn your computer into a weather information station. Among the available products are:

Software (programs) for forecasting weather, keeping records, charting storm tracks, and graphing weather data.

Data sets, on disk, of all sorts of climate records. A single floppy disk can hold decades of daily temperatures and rainfall for your favorite weather station, and a single optical disk—the computer equivalent of musical compact disks—can contain decades of daily climate data for thousands of weather stations. For more about this, write: National Climatic Data Center, Federal Building, Asheville, NC 28801-2696, or EarthInfo, Inc., 5541 Central Ave., Boulder, CO 80301-2846.

Bulletin board services you can dial up (if you have a modem to connect your computer to the telephone) for national and global weather data and forecasts. Some bulletin boards allow you to receive weather maps and satellite photos on your computer, and there are similar services that will print the maps on a facsimile machine.

New computer products appear nearly every day, so check the ads in the *Bulletin of the American Meteorological Society, American Weather Observer,* or *Weatherwise.*

WEATHER INSTRUMENTS

Of course, you want to set up a weather station in your back yard. Whether you go for the basics—a home-made, tin-can rain gauge and a household thermometer—or a fancy computerized set-up that even records the amount of ozone in the air depends on the depth of your interest and of your wallet. Some of the more common instruments, like thermometers, barometers and rain gauges, are carried by department and hardware stores. Radio Shack carries several electronic weather instruments. For a wider selection, try the catalogs available from the following suppliers.

American Weather Enterprises, P.O. Box 1383, Media, PA 19063

Edmund Scientific, 101 E. Gloucester Pike, Barrington, NJ 08007
Robert E. White Instruments, 34 Commercial Wharf, Boston, MA 02110
Science Associates, 31 Airpark Road, Box 230, Princeton, NJ 08542
Weathertrac, P.O. Box 122, Cedar Falls, IA 50613
Weatherwise Books and Instruments, Main Street, New London, NH 03527
Wind & Weather, P.O. Box 2320, Mendocino, CA 95460

More specifically, the best rain gauges for their respective prices are the plastic "wedge" made by Tru-Chek, Albert Lea, MN 56007, for under $10, and the $26.95 gauge sold by the American Weather Observer, 401 Whitney Blvd., Belvidere, IL 61008. Most commercial lightning detectors are dreadfully expensive, but you can buy one that picks up lightning 50 miles away for under $50 (that's less than $1 per mile!) from McCallie Manufacturing Corp., P.O. Box 17721, Huntsville, AL 35810.

One dandy little weather instrument that money can't buy is a thing called a "hail pad." Hail is as infrequent as it is important, and it's easy to miss a hail event by simply being away at work, in the basement, or asleep when it happens. The solution is a hail pad, which is nothing more than a slab of beaded styrofoam (like the stuff cheap picnic coolers are made of) wrapped in heavy-duty aluminum foil. Set it outside, weigh down the edges with bricks to keep it from blowing away, and when hail strikes, the cratered surface of the pad vividly records the storm. This dirt-cheap device was perfected by researchers in Illinois, who found it more reliable than high-tech gizmos with lasers and sound recorders. If your hail measures three-quarters of an inch or more in diameter, call the Weather Service immediately—stones that large are considered "severe weather" and potentially damaging, and forecasters want to know about it. If you find a hailstone 17 inches or more in circumference, put it in your freezer and protect it with your life—you may have the Hope Diamond of meteorology!

ASK THE EXPERTS

Sometimes you can get literature about the weather from various outfits that deal with the subject. Among these are your local Weather Service and the Agriculture or Meteorology departments at colleges and universities. Some local TV stations have pamphlets about weather. The National Center for Atmospheric Research, P.O. Box 3000, Boulder, CO 80303, is in the forefront of weather research, and their Information Office has some interesting public relations blurbs.

CLUBS, SOCIETIES & OTHER GROUPS

Meteorologists like to whoop it up just like everyone else, and have their own groups for doing so. I've already mentioned the American Meteorological Society, 45 Beacon Street, Boston, Mass. 02108, which appeals mostly to professionals. However, there are local chapters of the A.M.S. that welcome the public at their meetings. It's a good place to meet some meteorologists and enjoy interesting presentations. For information, write to the A.M.S. in Boston or to the closest local chapter:

Twin Cities A.M.S. Chapter, c/o Bruce Watson, 2514 Brenner St., Roseville, MN 55372 (while you're at it, ask Bruce about the local chapter of the American Association of Weather Observers);

Western Wisconsin A.M.S. Chapter, c/o Jim Crowley, WKBT-TV, 141 South 6th St., LaCrosse, WI 54601;

Lake Agassiz A.M.S. Chapter, c/o Fred Remer, Dept. of Atmospheric Sciences, University of North Dakota, Box 8216, University Station, Grand Forks, ND 58202-8216;

Sioux Valley A.M.S. Chapter, c/o Rollin E. Mannie, National Weather Service Forecast Office, 1 Weather Lane, Sioux Falls, SD 57104-0198.

If the aurora and eclipse chapters were your favorite parts of this book, maybe you should join one of Minnesota's astronomy clubs. The largest is the Minnesota Astronomical Society, affiliated with the Science Museum of Minnesota in St. Paul; call their recording at 612-643-4092 for more information. Other groups are:

Arrowhead Astronomical Society (Duluth), 218-726-7129; Fargo–Moorhead Astronomical Club, c/o Robert Brummond, P.O. Box 28, Concordia College, Moorhead, MN 56562;

Minnesota Valley Amateur Astronomers, c/o Roger Dier, Rte. 4, Box 15A, New Ulm, MN 56073;

North Star Astronomy Club, c/o David Starkka, 606 S. 8th St., Brainerd, MN 56401;

LaCrosse Area Astronomical Society, c/o Robert Allen, P.O. Box 2041, LaCrosse, WI 54602.

LAST BUT NOT LEAST

Reading *Minnesota Weather,* and every other weather book, from cover to cover, subscribing to all the weather magazines and climate reports, buying a barometer and a weather radio, and joining all the meteorological societies will not make you—or anyone—an expert on the weather. As Yogi Berra said, "You can observe a lot by just watching," and the way to become a weather expert is to watch it—frequently! So don't forget to look out your window once in a while. Take note of the changing clouds, the ups and downs of the thermometer, and (when it's clear) the northern lights. Put your boots on and stick a ruler in the snow. And be sure to write down your observations so you can read them years later. You'll find patterns to your local weather that no one could have ever told you about, and you'll find the total disregard the weather can often have for those patterns. After 10 or 20 years you might have some idea of what people mean by "climate change." Above all, you'll begin to understand and appreciate the weather like an old friend—a friend that always is there!

Index

■■■■■■■■■■■■■■■■■■■■■■■■■■■■■■

Richard A. Keen received a doctorate in climatology from the University of Colorado in 1979, and is self-employed as a writer/photographer specializing in weather. He has worked as a tornado spotter and forecaster, a storm meteorologist and a shortwave radio monitor, and is the author of *Skywatch: The Western Weather Guide* and *Skywatch: The Eastern Weather Guide,* both published by Fulcrum Press.